Last Chance Financial Planning Guide

Last Chance Financial Planning Guide

It's Not Too Late to Plan for Your Retirement If You Start Now

Anthony Spare with Paul Ciotti

PRIMA PUBLISHING

PRIMA PUBLISHING and colophon are registered trademarks of Prima Communications, Inc.

Figures by Matthew Zuck and Robin Lane

Library of Congress Cataloging-in-Publication Data
Spare, Anthony E.
    Last chance financial planning guide : it's not too late to plan for your retirement if you start now / Anthony Spare with
Paul Ciotti
        p.   cm.
    Includes index
    ISBN 0-7615-0836-8
    1. Finance, Personal. 2. Aged—Finance, Personal.
3. Investments. 4. Retirement income. I. Ciotti, Paul. II. Title.
HG179.S55278   1997
332.024—dc21   96-39642
                                                                        CIP

97 98 99 00 01 HH 10 9 8 7 6 5 4 3 2
Printed in the United States of America

How to Order
Single copies may be ordered from Prima Publishing, P.O. Box 1260BK, Rocklin, CA 95677; telephone (916) 632-4400. Quantity discounts are available. On your letterhead, include information concerning the intended use of the books and the number of books you wish to purchase.

Visit us on-line at http://www.primapublishing.com

*Dedicated to Art Laffer and Jude Wanniski,
who created a different way of thinking
about economics, and to Ronald Reagan
and Margaret Thatcher, who put their ideas
into practice for the world to see.*

Note to the Reader

Throughout this book, the performance results and composite port-folios of Spare, Kaplan, Bischel & Associates' clients are cited. These performance results reflect the reinvestment of dividends and earnings. Gross performance data does not reflect the deduction of investment advisory fees. Past performance is no guarantee of future results. Actual results may differ from composite results depending on the size of the account, investment objectives and/or restrictions, the amount of each transaction and related costs, the timing of when an account is opened, and other factors.

The results represented reflect the performance of all Spare, Kaplan, Bischel & Associates' clients who are invested using our Val-uePlus Equity strategy. Spare, Kaplan, Bischel & Associates' management believes that the performance quoted was generated by an investment philosophy and methodology similar to that described in this book. Future investments, however, will be made under different economic conditions and in different securities than those used by Spare, Kaplan, Bischel & Associates during the time discussed herein. Furthermore, the performance discussed herein reflects investments made for a limited period of time, and does not reflect performance in different economic or market cycles. It should not be assumed that future investors will experience returns, if any, comparable to those discussed herein. The information given is his-toric and should not be taken as any indication of future performance. Clients invested in strategies other than ValuePlus Equity will have had different investment results.

The performance of specific securities is discussed throughout the book. It should not be assumed that Spare, Kaplan, Bischel & Associates would make an identical recommendation today regarding any security, or that recommendations made in the future will be profitable or equal the performance of the securities discussed.

In this book we refer to certain company clients. They represent all of our corporate and mutual fund clients with over $75 million in assets under management who have given us permission to disclose their identities. It is not known whether the listed clients approve or disapprove of Spare, Kaplan, Bischel & Associates or the advisory services provided.

Contents

Caveats and Admonitions

A message to all you young people—don't worry about us old folks over fifty. The next thirty years will be our highlight years. Perhaps when we reach our eighties, we can talk about resting on our laurels a bit. We certainly are not going to be a burden on you. Just make sure you are not a burden on us.

Acknowledgments

For whatever insights and clear thinking there are in this book, I am indebted to my colleagues and associates at Spare, Kaplan, Bischel & Associates. I hesitate to name them for fear of leaving someone out, but their contributions both to this book and to my own thinking about investment management have been immense. The errors, I'm afraid, are mine.

The Search for Easter

Several years ago Harry B. Ernst, a Tufts professor of business statistics under whom I had studied nearly thirty years previously, came by our offices in San Francisco to make a pitch for his stock advisory service. He said he didn't remember me as a student, but in light of the fact that I had been enough of a success to go out and start an investment management company, he figured that I had most likely been a B student.

Well, I had been, and when I asked him how he knew, Ernst told me that in his experience A students tended to believe everything their professors said, which is how they got their A's in the first place. But it was the B students who had more success in the real world because they always questioned everything.

It's not often that something you learn in college changes your philosophy of life, but Ernst's business statistics course was one of them. In the first week of the course, Ernst talked about the difference between correlation and causality. He pointed out that the number of ordained ministers and the number of alcoholics were highly correlated even though there was no causal relationship.

Later we were assigned to correlate steel industry production with newspaper help-wanted ads. Other students would write elaborate reports, which I would then critique by saying that the data did not convey any relevant information. We had been having all these strikes in the steel industry. As a result, the unemployment data was meaningless, even though one could occasionally get some very nice correlations.

But it was the search for Easter that really turned on the light over my head. One day Ernst handed out monthly sales statistics for the previous ten or twenty years. Then he asked, "What was the seasonal adjustment factor every month?"

I did the problem straight ahead statistically—we didn't use slide rules or calculators—and it was a big job. You first had to figure the growth trend, subtract that, and then do a percentage each month of the detrended sales numbers. Everyone in the class, including me, got it wrong. The sole exception was one boy whose dad was a high official in the May Company, and thus he knew something about retail sales. I'll never forget this—he was sitting two rows in front of me—and when Ernst came around asking for our answers, this kid stood up and said, "You can't solve the problem unless you know the date of Easter."

Suddenly the light went on in my head—"Whoa!" We had been trying to solve a problem that couldn't be solved—despite all the data we had, we were still missing a key piece. Back in 1958 and 1959, which was when I took the course, there were no big discount outlets to compete with department stores. Because Easter finery was a big deal in those days, the department stores always had a huge sales increase at Easter. The problem was Easter can occur either in March or April each year, thus making the sales increase move too. There was no way to calculate a valid seasonal adjustment factor unless you also knew the date for Easter.

"Now that," I said to myself, "is really very interesting!"

I had always been naturally skeptical of numbers and statistics. But this really hammered it home—the real world is far too complex to be explained with nonintuitive, rote, straightline thinking. You can't explain the economy. You can't explain the stock market. And most importantly of all in the investment business, you can't consistently get a higher-than-average rate of return at lower-than-average risk unless you screen out the noise and focus on the factors that really matter, which is why I say I've always been in search of Easter.

It's an outlook that's taken me down quite different paths from most investment advisors over these last thirty years. More importantly, it's an outlook that helped me devise an individual investment strategy that is tailor-made for today's middle-aged baby boomers.

If you're like most middle-aged Americans, you are probably just now beginning to think seriously about retirement. And when you do, what you see alarms you—Social Security is in big trouble, your pension plans are inadequate, and your personal savings don't begin to cover your retirement needs. Well, from my point of view, there's no need to panic. You still have plenty of time to catch up—provided you take responsibility for your retirement and begin planning for it now.

I have on occasion been called relentlessly optimistic, but frankly it's an adjective I eagerly embrace. *Last Chance Financial Planning Guide* does for the typical baby boomer what my firm does for our private clients—show how to cope with the coming Social Security crunch, prepare a financial plan, build a portfolio, and use our firm's personal Relative Dividend Yield strategy to find those deceptively humble but high-returning stocks that provide long-term financial security. It's worked time and time again for our clients and—provided you follow the precepts—it will also work for you.

CHAPTER 1

———〜〜〜———

The New Face
of Retirement

By the time most people reach their middle forties, they realize—sometimes with an uncomfortable jolt—that they need to think about retirement. If you've picked up this book, you are probably one of them. You've got lots of questions, but why should you trust me to have the answers?

For over thirty years, I have managed pension assets and provided personal financial counseling to individuals and institutional investors. In 1989, I cofounded the San Francisco–based investment firm of Spare, Kaplan, Bischel & Associates, where I am chairman and chief investment officer. The firm has approximately $2.5 billion under our management and boasts such blue-chip clients as J.C. Penney and the Vanguard Equity Income Fund, among others. I have served as a past president of the Security Analysts of San Francisco, and I am a longtime member of such organizations as the Association of Investment Management and Research, the Institute of Chartered Financial Analysts, and the National Association of Business Economists. I've also pioneered an investment discipline I employ daily, which you'll become familiar with in this book, that I call Relative Dividend Yield (RDY). Five years ago, I wrote a book on the subject, entitled *RDY: Common Stock Investing for Income and Appreciation,* (John Wiley & Sons, 1992).

I'm not telling you this just to blow my own horn. When it comes to advice concerning your retirement money, you want someone with a pretty clear view of the territory. I wouldn't be writing this book if I didn't think I could provide that.

The premise of this book is that from here on out traditional retirement will not exist as a viable option for most people. The social experiment of retirement has failed and a new consensus is taking its place—all Americans should have the option of working as long as they can work, want to work, or need to work. From today on, old age won't so much mean bass fishing, shuffleboard, and bingo as it will mean a second career. This shouldn't be a hardship or any deep psychological blow (a recent Luntz poll found that twice as many people between the ages of eighteen and thirty-four believe in flying saucers as believe they will receive Social Security benefits). People now in their fifties will both live longer and be more productive at every stage of their lives than their parents or grandparents. This isn't hyperbole. It's the actuarial truth.

As for the notion that older workers need to retire (the sooner the better) in order to make room for younger ones, that is a kind of zero-sum, union-hall socialism pushed by British intellectuals in the thirties and totally discredited by the American experience ever since. If people over fifty were suddenly to retire, it wouldn't so much help the economy as send it into a tailspin.

Far from being some superfluous group taking up space and holding up the advancement of younger, more qualified people, older working Americans have more skills, better

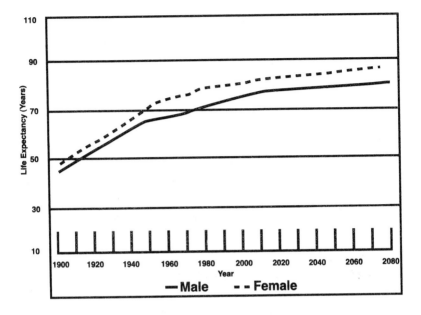

Year	Male	Female
1900	46.4	49.0
1910	50.1	53.6
1920	54.5	56.3
1930	58.0	61.3
1940	61.4	65.7
1950	65.6	71.1
1960	66.7	73.2
1970	67.2	74.9
1980	69.9	77.5
1990	71.6	78.7
* 2000	72.6	79.7
2010	74.1	80.5
2020	74.8	81.2
2030	75.4	81.8
2040	76.0	82.4
2050	76.6	83.0
2060	77.1	83.5
2070	77,7	84.1
2080	78.2	84.6

*All figures dated 2000 and beyond are projections.
Source: Life Tables for the United States Social Security
Area 1900–2080, Actuarial Study No. 107.

Figure 1.1   Life Expectancy at Birth

judgment, and even in many cases greater adaptability than their juniors. In part, this results from the plummeting effectiveness of the American education system—in recent years public schools simply haven't turned out graduates capable of competing with earlier generations when it comes to fundamental knowledge, work ethic, and learning skills (and no school can turn out graduates with the kind of wisdom that only comes with age and experience).

Other factors that make us more desirable employees are better health care and our rapidly increasing life spans. Unlike people sixty or eighty years ago, we're not being cut down by sickness and infirmity in what should be our most productive and effective years. It's true we don't have the stamina of younger folks (though we have far more than people our age used to have), but modern technology has eliminated a lot of the need for physical strength anyway. In the meantime, communications technology has reduced our dependence on stressful, exhausting daily commutes, allowing us to live where we want to and to work at our own pace.

And we will have to work. Social Security will start paying out more money than it takes in just three years after the oldest members of the baby boomer generation retire in 2011. Compared to fifty years ago, there are too few workers and too many retirees. To keep the system afloat, the government will have to cut benefits, raise taxes, or increase the age of retirement (mostly likely it will do all three). While this could be a major hardship for those who don't prepare, those of us willing and able to take control of our lives may not even notice the bump in the road.

Because we are both living longer and remaining healthier at any given age than all previous generations, we still have a long enough time horizon out in front of us to reap the benefits of appreciation and compounding in whatever assets we invest in—provided we take the attitude that it's our money and our responsibility to invest it as we see fit.

The specific details of our retirement plans are less important than the fact that we assume responsibility for ourselves and then follow through by staying on top of the factors—inflation, tax rates, asset allocation, and investment returns—that critically influence portfolios. As the Social Security debacle has demonstrated, we can't rely on the government to look out for our interests or our assets.

It isn't a matter of which political party is in power either. Both the Republicans and the Democrats have more than demonstrated their ability to take perfectly sound economies and toss them in the toilet. But even politicians can't deflect the overall trend forever—despite some detours along the way, we are inexorably moving toward a continually growing, low-tax, free-market economy. Socialist premiers and Third World dictators around the world now understand that they can't compete with us economically. Their totalitarian economies increasingly have been transformed into western-style, market-driven ones.

In this country, no matter what redistributive scheme the government puts into place, if it runs counter to the desire of most Americans to do business with one another without government interference, the people will find a way around it. The federal government can raise taxes; it can restrict competition; it can impose layer upon layer of regulation, repressing, suppressing, and distorting the economy, but it can't hold down the market forever. Sooner or later the market always wins. Even the far left now understands that we can never return to the 90 percent (or 70 percent or 60 percent) tax rates of the early post–World War II era.

I hope this news seems as good to those of you over fifty as it does to me. The more efficient, productive, and adaptable our economy becomes, the more it needs people with the ability to focus on problems, carry through projects, nurture worker relationships, and enthusiastically tackle the work at hand. These abilities have always been the hallmark of successful people (and companies and countries too). These are the people who will make sure that the 21st century won't be the dismal, resource-poor era predicted for us in the Club of Rome's 1972 report, "Limits to Growth," as it will be an opportunity for us, the generation over fifty, to thrive and contribute to society in ways that for previous generations were only open to the privileged few.

From here on out, the over-fifty generation will have the same impact that people 100 years ago had when they were in their thirties and forties, which is to say, working and competing full tilt in the vital center of the American economy.

Quick Test: You Probably Shouldn't Be Reading This Book if You Score Over Five

1. *The government will take care of my retirement:*

5	3	1
Agree	Not Sure	Disagree

2. *I currently have a net worth over $50 million:*

5	1
Agree	Disagree

3. *I am fifty years old, penniless, and jobless, but I buy so many lottery tickets that sooner or later one of them is bound to hit:*

5	3	1
Agree	Not Sure	Disagree

4. *I am currently ninety years old, ill, and will not live another three months:*

5   1

Agree   Disagree

5. *My job is secure and the company I work for will take care of my retirement:*

5   3   1

Agree   Not Sure   Disagree

The Case Against Social Security

First the bad news:

- Social Security is *not* an insurance policy, just age-determined welfare payments.

- There is *no* Social Security trust fund.

- Social Security is not so much a retirement plan as a Ponzi scheme where the current workers pay the retired.

- There cannot be any real benefit increases.

Despite the way the government has presented Social Security to the American people over the last sixty years, it has never been a real pension plan. The government didn't invest the money that people paid into it into any kind of trust fund (which could easily have been done had the plan been privatized from the beginning). Instead, the government took the money that came in, used part of it to pay off current retirees, and spent the rest running the government. Social Security isn't so much a pension plan as a huge flat tax. It has also increasingly become the dominant source of federal revenue—most workers pay more in payroll taxes than they do in income taxes.

Although this borders on massive fraud (any CEO who tried to run such a scheme on his company's employee pension plan today would end up in criminal court), the recognition of this problem has only recently sunk in for politicians and the people.

As late as 1950 there still were sixteen workers for every person collecting benefits. But because of steadily falling birthrates, earlier retirements (the percentage of workers who report that they work after age sixty-five has dropped from 46 percent in 1950 to about 15 percent today),[1] and increasing life spans (up 56 percent when measured from birth over the last 100 years), the ratio of workers to retirees has fallen so sharply that today there are only three workers for every person collecting benefits (and this will fall to two workers per retiree by 2030).[2] If nothing were to be done, the system would start running in the red by 2013 (two years after the first baby boomers start to retire) and be massively in debt by 2030 (see Table 1.1).[3]

One reason for the problem: people who joined the system decades ago get back far more from Social Security than they and their employers ever contributed in Social Security

---

1. C. Eugene Steuerle and Jon M. Bakija, *Retooling Social Security for the 21st Century* (New York, The Urban Institute Press, 1994), page 43, quoting Office of the Actuary (1993:247) and U.S. Bureau of Labor Statistics (1989 and 1972).

2. Mortimer Zuckerman, "Recognizing the Shades of Gray," *U.S. News & World Report,* May 13, 1996, page 96.

3. Ed Crane, "Privatizing Social Security," *Vital Speeches,* March 15, 1966, page 343.

Table 1.1 Growth in Elderly Population and Its Impact on the
Social Security System

Year	Persons Over 65 as a Percentage of U.S. Total
1950	8.0
1970	9.7
1990	12.3
2010*	12.9
2030	19.9
2050	20.8

* All figures dated 2000 and beyond are projections.

SOURCE: Board of Trustees, OASDI (1993) historical data and intermediate projections. From *Retooling Social Security for the 21st Century*
by Eugene Steuerle and Jon M. Bakija. Urban Institute Press, Washington, D.C.

taxes. The average one-earner couple from that time will get
about $123,000 more from Social Security than the couple
ever paid into it, and this includes interest on the couple's
contributions. If you throw Medicare into the pie, the windfall rises to over $300,000.[4]

This is an untenable burden on young people. A typical
young couple with one child earning $30,000 a year pays over
$7,000 a year in taxes (when you include the employer's FICA
contribution), while a typical retired couple with the same
income only pays $790 a year.[5]

---

4. Peter G. Peterson, "Will America Grow Up Before It Grows Old?" *The
Atlantic Monthly*, May 1996, page 55.

5. Ibid.

Table 1.2   Federal Tax Receipts, 1950–1991, As a Percentage of GDP

Year	Social Security	All Other Federal	Total Federal	Social Security Taxes as a Percentage of Total Federal Taxes
1950	1.1	15.4	16.5	6.8
1955	1.6	15.7	17.3	9.3
1960	2.5	15.3	17.8	13.8
1965	2.6	14.1	16.7	15.6
1970	3.9	14.1	18.0	21.9
1975	4.9	12.2	17.1	28.5
1980	5.3	13.5	18.7	28.1
1985	6.0	11.7	17.7	34.0
1990	6.6	11.9	18.5	35.8
1991	6.8	11.4	18.1	37.3

SOURCE: Calculations by Eugene Steuerle and Jon M. Bakija based on data from the U.S. Bureau of Economic Analysis. From *Retooling Social Security for the 21st Century* by Steuerle and Bakija, Urban Institute Press, Washington, D.C.

There has been much talk in recent years of reforming or privatizing Social Security. But this would require more courage than politicians of either party have shown to date. In the words of Cato Institute president Ed Crane, Social Security hasn't just been a sacred cow, it has also been the fatal "third rail" of electoral politics—"touch it and your career was over!"

As a result, the Social Security tax rate as a percentage of GDP has gone up 518 percent since 1950 and now accounts for over 37 percent of all federal tax receipts (see Table 1.2). There's no way this can continue, which is why I say, if you intend to depend on Social Security for your old age, you are living in a dreamworld, banking on promises that the government cannot keep. There's only one way to guarantee you have a comfortable and secure old age and that's to provide for it yourself.

You're Going to Live Longer, Make More Money

Now, the good news.

Although Social Security isn't going to be there for you, it's no big deal—you're going to live longer, be healthier, and make more money than your parents' generation (see Figure 1.2).

At the turn of the century, a man who was fifty could only expect to live till age seventy. Today, if you are a fifty-year-old male, you can expect to live to seventy-nine. With women, the differences are even larger: A woman who was fifty in 1900 could expect to live to seventy-two. Today, she can expect to live to eighty-five.

Life expectancy from birth for men has increased from forty-six in 1900 to about seventy-two today. For women it's gone from forty-nine to eighty. Furthermore, the longer you live, the greater your projected life span (see Figure 1.3). If you are a man and you get to age seventy-five, you can expect to live to eighty-four. If you get to eighty-four, you can expect to live to ninety. If you get to ninety, you can expect to live to ninety-four. (A ninety-year-old woman can expect to live to about ninety-five.)

Early Retirement: An Experiment That Didn't Work

For most previous generations, retirement was what we did for those few short years between quitting work and going to our graves. Then the prosperity of post–World War II America came along and gave people the option of retiring at an early age, working part time, or choosing not to work at all. Today, it's clear that most people will have to work longer than our parents' generation did. On the other hand, it will almost certainly be at more interesting and stimulating occupations than our parents ever enjoyed.

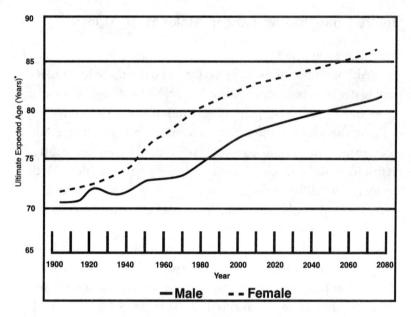

Year	Male	Female
1900	70.5	71.5
1910	70.6	72.1
1920	71.7	72.5
1930	71.3	73.2
1940	71.6	74.3
1950	72.7	76.5
1960	72.9	77.8
1970	73.2	79.0
1980	74.9	80.6
1990	76.1	81.2
** 2000	77.0	81.9
2010	77.7	82.5
2020	78.3	83.0
2030	78.8	83.6
2040	79.4	84.1
2050	79.9	84.6
2060	80.3	85.1
2070	80.8	85.6
2080	81.3	86.1

*Ultimate Expected Age equals age plus life expectancy.

**All figures dated 2000 and beyond are projections.

Source: Life Tables for the United States Social Security
Area 1900–2080, Actuarial Study No. 107.

Figure 1.2   *Ultimate Expected Age at Fifty: In Years, Given Year
When Age Fifty*

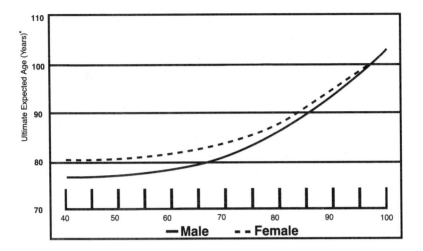

Age	Male	Female
40	74.8	80.5
45	75.3	80.8
50	76.1	81.2
55	77.0	81.9
60	78.2	82.7
65	79.8	83.8
70	81.8	85.2
75	84.1	87.0
80	87.0	89.1
85	90.2	91.6
90	93.9	94.7
95	97.9	98.3
100	102.2	102.5

*Ultimate Expected Age equals age plus life expectancy.
SOURCE: Life Tables for the United States Social Security
Area 1900–2080, Actuarial Study No. 107.

Figure 1.3   *Ultimate Expected Age, 1990: In Years, Given Age in 1990*

If you feel any impulse to lament your lost early retirement, you may want to take a few seconds to throttle it in its bed right now. For most of us, it is our work that gives meaning to our lives. Retirement is a failed concept that, except for the post–World War II era, hasn't existed any time in our history. Prior to that most people worked as long as they had a job and were healthy enough to do it. The notion that we should all retire at age sixty-five is a political decision—not a medical, scientific, or economic one. Just because German Chancellor Otto von Bismarck seized on sixty-five as the mandatory retirement age in Germany in 1889 (when average life expectancy from birth was just forty-five years) doesn't mean we have to use the same number today.

For one thing, we don't all suddenly quit functioning after sixty-five. That's not a magic age after which our energy and abilities suddenly decline. There is no reason to expect a seventy-year-old person today to act and feel the same way a seventy-year-old did fifty years ago. People really don't change that much between fifty-five and seventy-five anyway. This is why I say the notion of doing certain things at certain ages is rapidly disappearing. From here on out, it will be increasingly common to make decisions not on age but on proportions of one's life. You'll spend perhaps the first quarter of your life getting an education, the next third in your first career, the following third in your second career, and your final 6 percent (perhaps five years) in retirement (see Table 1.3).

If you are only just now turning fifty, you're in the prime of life with a good thirty to thirty-five years ahead of you. In fact, these may very well be your best years. For the most part, the pressure is off. Your liabilities most likely are going down and your income is still going up. The house is paid for. The kids are through college and on their own (or soon will be). Now you have both the time and the money to travel, to go

Table 1.3 Years and Percentage of Life Spent at Major Activities

| | 1900 | | 2000 | |
	Years	Percent	Years	Percent
School	14	25%	20	25%
First Career	40	73%	25	31%
Second Career	0	0%	30	38%
Retirement	1	2%	5	6%
Total	55	100%	80	100%

fishing, do what you've always wanted to do—but unlike some members of previous generations you will be doing a lot more than just passing time with watercolors or ceramics. Now you will have a choice. And for many of you that choice will be to keep actively involved in something that engages you, that society regards as valuable, and that rewards you for your effort. In other words—work.

When I say you are going to have to work past what has been the normal retirement age I am not, by the way, proposing any dramatic shift in the nation's work habits. Many people on Social Security are already working past what we consider normal retirement age. The first part of the year they work and report their income. Then when they get up against the maximum income allowable by Social Security, they quit reporting their income and work the rest of the year for cash.

It's an absurd system. No one else cares whether you earn income December 31 or January 1. Only the government worries about that sort of thing. In the meantime old folks, retirees, are out there moonlighting to earn cash under the table. The government just doesn't know about it, which is another reason the current Social Security system has to be dramatically reformed—it turns hard-working but needy old folks into crooks.

If people want to work longer, if they are capable of working longer, if there are employers eager to hire them, why not let them work as long as they want? These are experienced, capable people with a lot to offer society, not the least of which is a demonstrated commitment over the last thirty or forty years to getting the job done. If they want to continue working to provide for their old age, they deserve the chance. Certainly no one else is going to do it for them.

Beggar Thy Neighbor and Other Fallacies

Not everyone likes the idea of people working into their seventies. There is a whole school of thought that says we don't have the right to keep working forever, even if we can and want to. At some point, the argument goes, the older generation has a duty to sacrifice itself for the good of the country. Richard Lamm, when he was governor of Colorado, once gave a now infamous speech in which he asserted that old people had "a duty to die and get out of the way with all of our machines and artificial hearts and everything else like that and let . . . our kids . . . build a reasonable life."

Lamm has since furiously backpedaled from that speech, saying he was gravely misunderstood—he didn't mean that healthy old folks had a duty to get out of the way but only that we shouldn't spend thousands of dollars to artificially prolong the lives of terminally ill people for a desperate few extra days or weeks when the money could be spent so much more rationally on preventative health care for the young and productive.

Even so, in some circles, the notion still exists that old people, even if they are healthy and productive, have the duty to retire and make way for younger workers. This wouldn't be such a problem if people could depend on help from Social

Security. Since we can't, if we are going to make people retire at some point, we ought to make it conditional on performance, not age. A person's ability to do the job is so often independent of age anyway. I know feeble fifty year olds and incredibly dynamic eighty-five year olds. A lot of it is purely genetic. You want to have a long life? Choose parents who lived to a ripe old age.

We wouldn't even be talking about forcing older workers to make way for younger workers if it weren't for the Depression, an event so traumatic to the generations that lived through it that even today millions of Americans still believe that there are only so many jobs and so much money in the world and, as a corollary, that if younger workers are ever going to get their shot and their share, then older workers will have to retire voluntarily (or be made to by law).

In fact, as more and more people increasingly understand, the creation of jobs and wealth is not a zero-sum game in which every extra dollar in my pocket means one dollar less in yours. A lot of this kind of dismal thinking came out of English universities back in the thirties—the so-called "beggar-thy-neighbor" theory of economics. These socialist theoreticians made the mistake of thinking the economic pie was fixed—there was only so much money, only so many jobs, and the major task of society was to figure out how to divide up these limited resources in the most equitable way. Therefore corporations had to give up their profits and wealthy people had to surrender part of their income in order to spread the wealth around.

We finally began to get away from this when John Kennedy came along and pointed out what many economists already knew—"a rising tide lifts all boats." If countries follow the right policies, they grow. There isn't any fixed limit to prosperity in the world. Any country can become more wealthy, even as the countries around it become more wealthy too.

Right now China's economy is going through a tremendous economic boom, having surged 11.7 percent a year between 1990 and 1994.[6] But this doesn't mean the economies of all the other Pacific Rim countries have suddenly collapsed. They're growing simultaneously. Contrary to what the old-line socialists have always maintained, growth in one country doesn't come at the expense of growth in another.

Economist Jude Wanniski in *The Way the World Works* takes a look at countries around the world and shows how when the countries follow good policies they grow, and when they follow bad policies they don't. In one example he compares Ghana and the Ivory Coast, two side-by-side African countries, one of which prospers and one of which doesn't.

What is the difference between the two? Well, it's not the people. It's not the religion. It's not the climate. It's economic policy—one country rewards work and the other punishes it.

Can Work, Want to Work, Need to Work

Here it is in the most simple form: You will be able to work; you will want to work; you probably will have to work, either part-time or past what until now had been your expected retirement age.

With the ratio of working people to retirees plummeting, there will be no shortage of jobs for people with skill, experience, wisdom, and the ability to get along with other people.

---

6. China Statistical Yearbook, 1994.

One undeniable advantage seniors have over younger workers is their ability to take the long view of things. They're dependable, less likely to run off half-cocked and, since they've seen it all before, less inclined to get flustered under stress.

Although a lot of people might not agree, I also believe that in many cases older people are more adaptable. Unlike the generations that followed it, the fifties generation (people who were born at the end of World War II and grew up during the 1950s) learned how to learn. This doesn't mean we all will become creative geniuses in our old age. The great scientific breakthroughs, as always, will continue to be made by those much younger (they don't know what will not work). Our contribution will be organization and implementation—the younger generation will come up with the innovations and those of us over fifty will put them into practice.

Technology's Gift to People over Fifty

Although in former times people over fifty found it harder to compete with younger, stronger workers, technology has changed much of that. Machinery now does the heaving and lifting once done by younger men. You don't have to be twenty-three with big muscles and dig ditches all day in order to make a contribution. Technology multiplies your strength and extends your working life.

In the fields of communications and information technology, conditions change so fast that businesses have a hard time finding people to implement these new technologies. One might think that young people have an automatic advantage with new technology because they tend to pick up new things with greater ease. Although this might have been true in the past, it's not necessarily true anymore. Over the last couple of decades our schools haven't educated young people the same way we were educated.

Kids spend far more time in front of the television than they do reading books. Their attention spans are shorter. In response to demands for diversity the curriculum has been dumbed down and flattened out. Schools put so much emphasis on making kids feel good about themselves they don't *give* them anything to feel good about, such as a concrete knowledge of economics, history, or geography. On standardized math tests American students score worse than students in virtually any other industrialized country (but they feel better about it).

It isn't that our children aren't bright. It's that they lack knowledge and training and consequently require more supervision. They lack the big picture that previous generations absorbed automatically. Until this problem is solved, it provides a big opportunity for those of us over fifty to stay in the workforce—but this time on our own terms.

Everyone is aware of the impact on telecommuting of fax machines, e-mail, and computers. What you might not be aware of is the stunning impact that full-speed, full-frame, color video telephones will have on the way people work.

One reason many people retire early is that they are tired of living in cities full of noise, dirt, crime, and social unrest. They want a place with more amenities and less stress. People who are already living in the suburbs want to get away from stressful time-wasting hour-long commutes at the beginning and end of each day. They've been driving in rush-hour traffic for the last thirty years. They don't relish the idea of doing it for five, ten, or fifteen more. Full-speed, full-frame, full-color video telephones will make telecommuting a fully viable option.

I'm not talking about old-fashioned video conferencing, which we've had for years and which no one regards as anything more than minimally satisfactory. In video conferencing you go to a conference room, get connected by technicians to another office in another city or country, and have what passes for a meeting. It's awkward and artificial and I've never met anyone who thinks that a group telephone conversation with a herky-jerky black-and-white picture is any substitute for a normal face-to-face conversation.

What I'm talking about is the broadband cable transmission of images directly to the computer monitor on your desk. You sit alone in your office and talk privately to your clients, colleagues, friends, or family as if they were sitting on the other side of your desk. It's a full-speed, full frame, full-color, audio-visual experience that will totally change the way we look at the world.

Furthermore, thanks to the deregulation of the telephone industry, this technology is right around the corner. Face-to-face meetings will still be important, but people won't have to commute to the office five days a week. One or two days (during non-rush hours) might very well be enough. People can live where they want to. Because fewer employees will be coming into the central office on any given day, businesses will need less office space. Congested, crime-ridden urban centers will gradually empty out. Office buildings in the central city will go begging. Gas consumption will go down. Freeways will be less crowded.

For older people, this will be an incredible advantage. Instead of having to waste two or more hours a day in stressful commutes five days a week, we can be hard at work before we finish our morning coffee. If we do need to go into the office, it will be at a time convenient to us. In the meantime, we will be able to work wherever we choose. If we need to work past sixty-five, we'll be able to do so with much less stress and far less disruption than they ever thought possible.

The Retirement Option

Not everyone who is capable of working past sixty-five wants to do it. One of our firm's clients just retired. He's in his early fifties. His wife retired last year.

Why did he retire so young?

Well, as he says, "The fish are calling."

Will the fish still be calling six months from now?

I don't know. But if anyone earned the right to retire early, he did. His wife was one of the first people (aside from the founders themselves) to go to work for a new technology company. Then it was just a startup company. Today it has 6,000 employees. Because they both were paid in stock options they both became multimillionaires. Now they are living the American dream.

I know that lots of people would call them lucky, but they worked hard and studied hard. They could have spent all their time in a second-rate company. But the company attracted people who were hard-working. People like that make their own luck.

Can other people do what they have done?

Well, obviously I think it's possible or I wouldn't be writing this book. But I must say a lot more people think they can support themselves on their current savings than actually can. They sit in my office and say, "Gee, well if I put together so much per month from here on out, what do I have after ten or twenty years?" And we pull out the calculator and figure it out. And guess what? It usually turns out to be an amazing amount of money.

Unfortunately—and this is the shocker—it's still probably not enough. According to the actuarial tables, people who have reached the normal retirement age of sixty-five can reasonably expect to live another twenty to twenty-five years (and possibly a good deal longer). If you figure out how many asscts you need to generate the same income as you get from earning a salary, it turns out that it's quite a lot.

If you have a modest annual income of $60,000, you would need $1 million in assets earning 6 percent interest to generate the same amount. It takes a huge amount of assets to say, "The hell with this. I don't want to work anymore. I'm just going to live off my money."

So . . . how do you get that pile of assets, that more-than-amazing amount of money?

I thought you'd never ask.

CHAPTER 2

———∽◊∽———

How Much
Do You Need to Retire?

It is no simple matter to know how much money you will need for your retirement. It depends on many factors, including your goals, your liabilities, interest rates, the tax structure, the inflation rate, your health, your lifestyle, and the part of the country in which you live.

If you want to maintain the assets that you have at retirement, for personal security or to leave something to your family or to a charity, you will need a considerable nest egg. On the other hand, if you're willing to draw down your principal and sell your assets (such as your house), you can get by on much less.

Putting together a retirement plan takes a fair amount of time and a lot of hard thought (former Fidelity Fund manager Peter Lynch once complained that people spend more time planning for their vacation than they do for their retirement). If all you need at this time is a quick and dirty first approximation, you can do the calculations with a pen and a pad or pocket calculator. If you have a personal computer and an

Internet account you can access web sites that provide free on-line retirement calculators (such as Fidelity, the Vanguard Group, American Express, Money, and the Quicken Financial Network).

If you don't trust yourself to draw up a retirement plan, you can have a professional financial planner draw up one for you (in Chapter 8, I discuss how to choose a financial planner).

Finally, if you require a sophisticated, fine-tuned approach and you have access to a personal computer, you can draw up a plan yourself using commercial retirement planning software. (Many people prepare the plan themselves, then once they are thoroughly familiar with the concepts, take it to a professional planner for checking and refinement.) Intuit's Quicken Financial Planner is quite a sophisticated program. Microsoft makes one called Money. Some of the web sites sell their own retirement planning programs at low cost.

One big advantage of using commercial retirement planning software is that the better ones automatically calculate the consequences of varying tax rates, inflation rates, tax deferred versus fully taxable savings, life expectancies, and portfolio mixes. As you change such variables as your projected retirement age, expected return or inflation rate, the changes instantly ripple through every graph and table in your plan, giving you instantaneous feedback on the variable's impact. With the Quicken Financial Planner you can even ask the program to suggest a possible solution. If your expectations are unrealistic, given your particular goals or initial conditions, the program will tactfully advise you of that.

What's an unrealistic expectation?

Well, consider, for example, the expectations of someone we'll call Louise, a successful single professional woman who retired in 1996 at age sixty-five with a million-dollar portfolio of stocks, bonds, and cash on which she is currently getting a conservative post-retirement return of 6 percent.

Now to most of us this sounds pretty good. But not to Louise. She has always done a lot of traveling, entertaining, and art collecting. As a single woman, she doesn't have any children herself but she would like to give some money to her nieces and nephews while she's still alive. Altogether, she figures, her post-retirement expenses will run about $100,000 a year.

Where will the money come from?

At a 6 percent rate of return she will earn about $60,000 from her investments. Her Social Security (since she is already receiving it we'll plan on it being there for her) will bring in another $10,632. This still leaves her short by $29,368.

How will she make up the difference?

Well, the simplest way is to pull money out of her principal. This turns out to be a substantial amount. Louise doesn't just need $100,000 a year. She needs $100,000 a year in current purchasing power. At a 3 percent inflation rate, she runs out of money in the year 2006, her tenth year of retirement (see Table 2.1, which shows how the inflation rate affects the real value of savings). Since Louise expects to live until age ninety, she will have fifteen more retirement years that are not fully funded.

What can she do?

Well, she may want to cut back on her lifestyle. Assuming her health is good and her medical expenses routine, she might very well find it possible to get by on $90,000 a year, instead of $100,000. That will get her through the year 2008, still leaving her with thirteen underfunded retirement years.

What else?

Since she was earning a substantial amount of money ($100,000 a year before retirement), she might want also to

Table 2.1   Annuity Generated by Savings

Savings,	After-Tax Rate of Return					
$(000)s	4%	5%	6%	7%	8%	9%
50	$2.0	$2.5	$3.0	$3.5	$4.0	$4.5
100	$4.0	$5.0	$6.0	$7.0	$8.0	$9.0
150	$6.0	$7.5	$9.0	$10.5	$12.0	$13.5
250	$10.0	$12.5	$15.0	$17.5	$20.0	$22.5
500	$20.0	$25.0	$30.0	$35.0	$40.0	$45.0
750	$30.0	$37.5	$45.0	$52.5	$60.0	$67.5
1000	$40.0	$50.0	$60.0	$70.0	$80.0	$90.0
1500	$60.0	$75.0	$90.0	$105.0	$120.0	$135.0
2000	$80.0	$100.0	$120.0	$140.0	$160.0	$180.0
2500	$100.0	$125.0	$140.0	$175.0	$200.0	$225.0
5000	$200.0	$250.0	$300.0	$350.0	$400.0	$450.0

Real Annuity Generated by Savings (Inflation 3%)

Savings,	After-Tax Rate of Return					
$(000)s	4%	5%	6%	7%	8%	9%
50	$0.5	$1.0	$1.5	$2.0	$2.5	$3.0
100	$0.9	$1.9	$2.9	$3.9	$4.9	$5.9
150	$1.4	$2.9	$4.4	$5.9	$7.4	$8.9
250	$2.3	$4.8	$7.3	$9.8	$12.3	$14.8
500	$4.5	$9.5	$14.5	$19.5	$24.5	$29.5
750	$6.8	$14.3	$21.8	$29.3	$36.8	$44.3
1000	$9.0	$19.0	$29.0	$39.0	$49.0	$59.0
1500	$13.5	$28.5	$43.5	$58.5	$73.5	$88.5
2000	$18.0	$38.0	$58.0	$78.0	$98.0	$118.0
2500	$22.5	$47.5	$72.5	$97.5	$122.5	$147.5
5000	$45.0	$95.0	$145.0	$195.0	$245.0	$295.0

consider delaying her retirement for few more years. If she waited until age sixty-seven, for instance, and invested 5 percent of her $100,000 salary in her retirement portfolio, she wouldn't run out of money until 2011 (unfortunately this would still leave her with ten years yet to go—a $100,000-a-year lifestyle is a tough nut to crack). To fully fund that level of lifestyle, Louise would have to work till age seventy-three, and even that figure assumes an inflation rate of 3 percent. At high inflation rates, even saving quite a bit more doesn't help very much. If inflation went up to 4 percent, Louise would run out of money in 2018, three years before the end of her plan. Even if she doubled her savings rate from 5 percent to 10 percent, that would only fund her retirement plan till 2020, leaving her with a year to go and no money.

Another consideration: We have been assuming here that Louise will only live to ninety. That's a reasonable number for a sixty-five-year-old woman in good health today. But with a healthful lifestyle (and good genes), Louise might very well live to ninety-five or ninety-eight.

How can she provide for that?

Unless she wants to work for the better part of her retirement, Louise may have to consider cutting back her rather luxurious lifestyle, traveling less, buying less art, giving less money to her nieces and nephews. If Louise could reduce her annual expenses to $60,000 a year, she could retire at sixty-nine and still have $80,000 when she dies to leave to her heirs.

Would Louise be content with that?

I don't know. Retirement planning requires both flexibility and a rational ability to set priorities. Many people don't have those. One who did was a client of ours whom we'll call Stan.

When Stan first approached us a few years ago to help him draw up a retirement plan, he was fifty-five years old, suffering from cancer, and expecting to live no more than a year.

Fortunately, he had $2 million in assets. His living expenses were $100,000 a year. Joy, his wife, fifty, enjoyed good health and could expect to outlive him by thirty-five years. Stan's goal was to provide an adequate income for her and to leave their children $1 million upon her death.

Our first question was whether Stan wanted to leave the children $1 million in current purchasing power or simply $1 million. One million dollars with the purchasing power of today's dollars would have meant setting aside $232,000 at an 8 percent rate of return (and assuming a 3 percent inflation rate). If Stan simply wanted to leave the nice round sum of $1 million, however, he had only to set aside $100,000 today. It would appreciate into $1 million by the time the children inherited it upon Joy's death.

After discussion, Stan decided he couldn't worry about maintaining current purchasing power for his children's inheritance. He set aside the $100,000 for the children and then had $1.9 million left to cover Joy's needs.

The actuarial tables said that Joy should live another thirty-five years, but we knew there was a 10 percent chance she might live as much as ten years longer than that, for a total of forty-five years. We decided this was the wiser number of years to plan for. Using a 3 percent inflation rate, we found she would run out of money after only twenty-seven years.

Something had to give. We asked Joy if she felt $100,000 a year in today's dollars was an absolute necessity. After some thinking, she estimated she could manage comfortably on $75,000 a year. This seemed to work. At this rate, Joy's money would last forty-five years and there would still be $1 million to give to the children. It was a scenario that everyone was happy with.

Now the good news. Although Stan's bone-marrow transplant didn't work, the doctors put him on a new experimental medication that put his cancer in full remission. Stan was doing so well he went back to work, this time as a marketing consultant. He calls us all the time. If he can earn enough to cover their current expenses, he will go a long way toward resolving any possible fears for his wife's welfare. But whatever Stan or Joy earns, it will be money that won't be removed from the investment account and thus will be compounding over time, adding to their portfolio, not reducing it.

Calculating Your Retirement Needs

Although some financial planners suggest that people should expect to see their expenses drop 10 to 20 percent after retirement, there really is no good way to predict how much money a client will need in retirement. With some people, expenses actually go up—either due to health problems or the retiree's greater freedom now to do whatever he or she wants. With other people, expenses drop dramatically, especially if they do something drastic, like sell their home in the city and move to rural Montana, where expenses are next to nothing.

How do you figure out what your expenses after retirement are going to be?

This is a tough item, because people tend to underestimate their expenses. To help you recall the big ticket items, you might want to gather together a year's worth of checks or credit card receipts. If it's been ten or twenty years since you remodeled the kitchen, did major house repairs, bought a new car, or replaced large appliances, you will need to budget for those in your retirement plan.

To be on the safe side when projecting your living expenses, you might want to increase them each year at the general inflation rate, even though for most retired people living expenses increase much slower than that.

For people who own personal computers, there are numerous inexpensive household budget programs on the market, including Quicken, Microsoft's Money, and Andrew Tobias's Managing Your Money. These allow you to characterize your expenses individually so that at the end of the year you can see what your annual expenses are by category.

Once you know how much money you need to live each year, you next have to figure out how many years your retirement income has to last. Refer to Figure 1.3, "Ultimate Expected Age 1990," on page 13. This will tell you what your expected life span is. If you currently are a fifty-year-old of the educated middle class, you can expect on average to live to age seventy-nine if you are a man and to eighty-five if you are a woman.

It's important to remember that these figures are averages. In the case of all the men aged fifty today, half will die before they reach seventy-nine and half will die later. To make sure that no one runs out of money in his or her retirement, we base our projections on the possibility that any given person might very well live two or three standard deviations beyond the actuarial average for everyone else his same age. This means that in the case of a man who is currently fifty years old, we plan on his living at least to eighty-five or ninety when we make our financial calculations (not just seventy-nine), and for a fifty-year-old woman we plan on her living at least to ninety or ninety-five (not just eighty-five). In cases where family members are extraordinarily long-lived (we have one client with a relative who lived to 105), we revise our estimates upward accordingly.

Once you know how much income you need each year for retirement and how many years you (or your spouse) is expected to live after retirement, then you can calculate how much money you need to have saved by the time you retire.

Suppose that you are fifty years old in 1997, earning $50,000 a year. After paying taxes and Social Security, you have $39,675 a year for living expenses. Assuming that you have saved $75,000, which you have invested in a balanced portfolio of 60 percent bonds and 40 percent large cap and international stocks, you can figure on a conservative, after-retirement rate of return of about 6 percent. Even if you don't add any more money to your retirement fund, when you retire in 2017 your taxable investments will be worth $161,786. Given a 3 percent inflation rate, this is not nearly enough.

Assuming that Social Security will provide you $14,456 a year, you will need an additional $25,119 a year from your portfolio (people who have many years to go before retirement might want to take a more conservative approach and not count Social Security at all). To make sure you don't run out of money before you die, we will plan on your needing an income at least to age eighty-three (if a man), which is to say for thirteen years after you retire. Assuming a conservative after-retirement rate of return of 6 percent, your assets will be depleted in 2021, with nine years still to go on your retirement plan.

What can you do?

Since you are employed, the easiest thing is to take advantage of your company's 401k tax-deferred retirement plan. If you invest a fairly modest 5 percent of your income, or $2,500 a year, in a tax-deferred retirement plan, thereby reducing your living expenses to $37,175 a year, you will have enough money to last you until 2024 (still leaving six years unfunded).

Since you probably don't want to reduce your standard of living even further and since you have no control over the inflation rate and only limited control on your after-retirement rate of return, the only other variable with significant impact is your retirement age. If you decide to delay your retirement to seventy-five instead of seventy, your portfolio at that time will be worth $413,228, which will last you to 2030 and still leave you with $79,019 to leave to your heirs.

What If I'm Fifty and Haven't Saved a Thing?

One, don't panic. You still have twenty-five years ahead of you to invest. You have a long time horizon. You made it to fifty, despite all the nonsense that you put yourself through when you were young. You are a survivor. Actuarially, if you are a fifty-year-old man today you will live to be seventy-nine (eighty-five if you're a woman), and you should really plan on living to be eighty-five or ninety. This will ensure you don't run out of money. The last thing you want to do is die owing even a *single* dollar.

Having a dollar and owing a dollar are totally different conditions. Even though it looks like only two dollars, they are worlds apart. You don't want to die owing people money. You want to make sure that your survivors' memory of you is not, "Boy he was a great old guy, but, damn, I had to pay for his funeral." You can work your whole life, be a loving parent and good provider, and that will take the edge right off.

Because you are going to live longer, you will need more money for your old age and this in turn means working longer than perhaps you had planned. If you haven't started saving, you won't be able to retire next year or at fifty-five or sixty or sixty-five.

On the other hand, if you're in good health, who the hell wants to retire anyway? Everyone is living longer and feeling better in the process. Assume you work until seventy or seventy-five. You can work by yourself. You can work upstairs, in the back yard, down the street. You can work for the same company you currently work for and go in once or twice a week and do everything else by computer, fax, and telephone.

Compounding is important. Not getting sucked into today's mania is important. Say your great aunt leaves you a load of cash—you don't have to invest it all today, but you probably should put something in. Aim to be fully invested in two years.

If you don't have any money saved, it's still not too late to start. You don't just have fifteen years. Most likely you have thirty to thirty-five years, and out of that you have at least twenty to twenty-five years to build assets. You can't do anything about yesterday anyway. You have to start today and just go ahead. (For projections on what your savings will earn you over your last working years, given a 10 percent rate of return, see Tables 2.2 and 2.3.)

Because these are your prime earning years, your income will likely grow between now and your final retirement date. Sometimes you will need that extra money for expenses; often you won't, which will give you an opportunity to *start saving now.*

The sooner you begin to earn interest on your savings, the better. Whenever you can, put it in IRA accounts and 401k plans. Go to the max on those, because they are tax deferred. You won't have to pay any capital gains or income taxes until you retire and presumably are in a lower tax bracket.

Start with whatever you can afford. Set specific goals and stick to them as if your life depended on them.

Table 2.2   Accumulation of Savings from Salary, Ten and Fifteen Years Before Retirement

Variables: Savings Rate, Salary
Constants: Years to Retirement—10; Rate of Return—10%

Salary, $(000)s				Savings Rate			
	5%	10%	15%	20%	25%	30%	35%
40	$35.1	$70.2	$105.3	$140.4	$175.5	$210.6	$245.7
60	$52.6	$105.2	$157.8	$210.4	$263.0	$315.6	$368.2
80	$70.1	$140.2	$210.3	$280.4	$350.5	$420.6	$490.7
100	$87.7	$175.4	$263.1	$350.8	$438.5	$526.2	$613.9
120	$105.2	$210.4	$315.6	$420.8	$526.0	$631.2	$736.4
140	$122.7	$245.4	$368.1	$490.8	$613.5	$736.2	$858.9
150	$131.5	$263.0	$394.5	$526.0	$657.5	$789.0	$920.5
200	$175.3	$350.6	$525.9	$701.2	$876.5	$1,051.8	$1,227.1
300	$263.0	$526.0	$789.0	$1,052.0	$1,315.0	$1,578.0	$1,841.0

Constants: Years to Retirement—15; Rate of Return—10%

Salary, $(000)s				Savings Rate			
	5%	10%	15%	20%	25%	30%	35%
40	$69.9	$139.8	$209.7	$279.6	$349.5	$419.4	$489.3
60	$104.8	$209.6	$314.4	$419.2	$524.0	$628.8	$733.6
80	$139.8	$279.6	$419.4	$559.2	$699.0	$838.8	$978.6
100	$174.7	$349.4	$524.1	$698.8	$873.5	$1,048.2	$1,222.9
120	$209.7	$419.4	$629.1	$838.8	$1,048.5	$1,258.2	$1,467.9
140	$244.7	$489.4	$734.1	$978.8	$1,223.5	$1,468.2	$1,712.9
150	$262.1	$524.2	$786.3	$1,048.5	$1,310.5	$1,572.6	$1,834.7
200	$349.5	$699.0	$1,048.5	$1,398.0	$1,747.5	$2,097.0	$2,446.5
300	$524.2	$1,048.4	$1,572.6	$2,096.8	$2,621.0	$3,145.2	$3,669.4

Table 2.3 Accumulation of Savings from Salary, Twenty and Twenty-Five Years Before Retirement

Variables: Savings Rate, Salary
Constants: Years to Retirement—20; Rate of Return—10%

Salary, $(000)s	5%	10%	15%	Savings Rate 20%	25%	30%	35%
40	$126.0	$252.0	$378.0	$504.0	$630.0	$756.0	$882.0
60	$189.0	$378.0	$567.0	$756.0	$945.0	$1,134.0	$1,323.1
80	$252.0	$504.0	$756.0	$1,008.0	$1,260.0	$1,512.1	$1,764.1
100	$315.0	$630.0	$945.0	$1,260.0	$1,575.1	$1,890.1	$2,205.1
120	$378.0	$756.0	$1,134.0	$1,512.1	$1,890.1	$2,268.1	$2,646.1
140	$441.0	$882.0	$1,323.1	$1,764.1	$2,205.1	$2,646.1	$3,087.1
150	$472.5	$945.0	$1,417.6	$1,890.1	$2,362.6	$2,835.1	$3,307.6
200	$630.0	$1,260.0	$1,890.1	$2,520.1	$3,150.1	$3,780.1	$4,410.2
300	$945.0	$1,890.1	$2,835.1	$3,780.1	$4,725.2	$5,670.2	$6,615.3

Constants: Years to Retirement—25; Rate of Return—10%

Salary, $(000)s	5%	10%	15%	Savings Rate 20%	25%	30%	35%
40	$216.4	$432.7	$649.1	$865.5	$1,081.8	$1,298.2	$1,514.5
60	$324.5	$649.1	$973.6	$1,298.2	$1,622.7	$1,947.3	$2,271.8
80	$432.7	$865.5	$1,298.2	$1,730.9	$2,163.6	$2,596.4	$3,029.1
100	$540.9	$1,081.8	$1,622.7	$2,163.6	$2,704.5	$3,245.5	$3,786.4
120	$649.1	$1,298.2	$1,947.3	$2,596.4	$3,245.5	$3,894.5	$4,543.6
140	$757.3	$1,514.5	$2,271.8	$3,029.1	$3,786.4	$4,543.6	$5,300.9
150	$811.4	$1,622.7	$2,434.1	$3,245.5	$4,056.8	$4,868.2	$5,679.5
200	$1,081.8	$2,163.6	$3,245.5	$4,327.3	$5,409.1	$6,490.9	$7,572.7
300	$1,622.7	$3,245.5	$4,868.2	$6,490.9	$8,113.6	$9,736.4	$11,359.1

Diversification is always important. You are always going to want some cash, some bonds, some stocks. Stocks earn the most money in the long run but in the short run they have the greatest volatility (fluctuations in value). So for protection you are going to want a little diversification, and for that mutual funds are a terrific vehicle. You just want to be sure you don't overdo it. A mutual fund by its nature is diversified. So you may want to look at a couple of styles of equity funds, maybe one bond fund, and one money market fund. That's more than enough. You can't reduce your risk by over-investing in mutual funds. It's far better to own a few funds that you can keep track of than many funds that you can't.

If you haven't started saving yet, don't delay any longer. According to *Newsweek* magazine financial columnist Jane Bryant Quinn, most members of the baby boomer generation only save about one-third of what they need to retire at the same lifestyle they currently enjoy.

That isn't going to do it. People in their prime earning years should save 10 to 15 percent of their gross income.

If you want the retirement you have been looking forward to, you are going to have to save and you are going to have to invest. Put something in the pot every payday. If you work for a company, arrange to have deductions made from your paycheck automatically. If you never see the money, you may not even miss it.

Most of all, don't waste your time regretting lost opportunities. You never want to play the "could have, would have, should have" game: "I could have bought IBM, or Microsoft, or Procter & Gamble. . . ." "I would have been a millionaire today. . . ." "I should have gotten into the market two years ago. If only I had bought Microsoft ten years ago. . . ."

That's spilt milk, water under the bridge. Don't waste time worrying over things that no one can change.

No one ever taught you retirement planning in high school or college. This is something you're going to have to do on your own. Get some advice, do some research, learn about IRAs, 401ks, stocks, bonds, mutual funds, market yield, and index funds. Master the techniques of market analysis presented in this book. If you have a computer, you will find that there are hundreds and hundreds of web sites with free investment and retirement information on the Internet. Some of the better ones are sponsored by major corporations and financial magazines such as American Express, *Barron's, Forbes, Fortune, Kiplingers,* Merrill Lynch, *Money,* the CNN Financial Network, Quicken Financial Network, and *U.S. News & World Report.* To get a list, search for "retirement planning" or "financial planning" with your web browser.

On-line services such as CompuServe and America Online also offer personal financial planning sites with articles and downloads and forums where members can ask questions, exchange information, and download files. Usenet newsgroups serve the same function on the Internet. The American Association of Individual Investors offers a vast amount of investment and/or retirement advice. Finally, for cheap-stock investing strategies, visit the Spare, Kaplan, Bischel & Associates web page (http://www.skbaweb.com).

—◦◦◦—

CHAPTER 3

—⁓⁓⁓—

Put Your Assets
to Work for You

The number of people who have never really added their assets up is astonishing. They add up all their bank accounts and forget their house or they leave out a major account entirely—"Damn, I forgot about that account. My aunt just gave me these stocks or those bonds."

As a result most people are both wealthier than they realize and wealthier than their income would seem to indicate. Sometimes they own shares in the company for which they work. Sometimes they have stock options or pension plans. Even when people think to include all their assets, they don't assess them at market value. If you bought your house twenty years ago, it is probably worth three to five times what you paid for it. Thirty years ago the Standard & Poor's Index of 500 was under 80. Today (the beginning of 1997) it's around 775. Stock returns have been doubling every five years for the last twenty years.

Compounding helps a lot. Many people who are fifty today started their business careers when they were around twenty. They've had thirty years of higher and higher incomes, thirty years of buying company stock or contributing to a pension plan, thirty years of compounding their assets. Under circumstances like these you don't need a super-high return to have a substantial amount of money, which is why I say there are far more millionaires in the world than most people realize.

A Survey of Portfolio Possibilities

If your goal is to accumulate enough money while you're still working so that you can retire in comfort and security, you have to start earning money for your retirement by investing wisely. Luckily, there is no shortage of asset types in which to invest your money: stocks, bonds, treasury bills, certificates of deposit, bank deposits, insurance policies, real estate, venture capital, and gold.

Each asset type has advantages and disadvantages. You don't want to get wedded to a single asset type. No one asset, or particular combination of assets, is appropriate for everyone.

Bank Deposits

It's always a good idea to keep three to six months' income in cash on hand for emergencies. But the interest rate paid by banks on savings accounts and certificates of deposit is so low that once inflation is factored in, you may actually end up losing purchasing power. Consider money market funds instead.

Certificates of Deposit

These are little more than an extension of savings accounts with minimal risk (and minimal return). These have set interest rates, set maturation dates, and heavy penalties for early withdrawal. Certificates of deposit are virtually risk free, but they have such low rates of return that the best you can do with them is match the rate of inflation.

Money Market Funds

The majority of funds in cash equivalents should be in money market funds. It's foolish to go for a few basis points higher yield. The underlying assets of your money market funds should be U.S. government obligations. If you are going to take risks, do it with your equity (stock) assets, not with your cash reserves.

Bonds

A bond is an IOU that an issuer (either a corporation or the government) gives to an investor. When you buy a bond, you may pay less than its face value. The bond pays interest monthly or semi-annually. Then at maturity, you can redeem the bond for its face value.

Bonds offer a higher and more reliable return than money market funds or bank savings accounts. But they offer less total return than stocks over the long haul. Traditionally, investors use bonds to diversify their portfolios. Stocks tend to be more volatile; bonds less so. Stocks and bonds tend to have an inverse relationship. When stocks are doing well, bonds do poorly. And vice versa.

Because retired people are generally more concerned about security than asset growth, they tend to prefer bonds.

Treasury Securities

Treasury securities are direct obligations of the Treasury of the United States. The government issues them as a means of borrowing money to meet official expenditures not covered by tax revenues. They include treasury bills and notes, and treasury bonds.

Treasury bills, also called T-bills, have maturities of ninety days to one year after issue. Although T-bills are virtually risk free (essentially they are the U.S. equivalent of gold), their rates of return usually just match the rate of inflation. T-bills should be part of the cash equivalent section of any portfolio. If you want to avoid the hassle of buying treasury bills yourself you can invest in money market funds that purchase treasury bills.

Treasury notes have maturities of one to ten years and treasury bonds have maturities of ten to thirty years. Either one offers good rates of return at relatively low risk and thus, in conjunction with common stocks, is a good way to diversify and thus protect your portfolio from sudden declines.

Stocks

Stocks are shares of the net income and assets of a corporation. They offer the best returns over the long run, with high liquidity (you can sell your shares at any time). They can be volatile, though, going through cycles of low and high total returns. For best results, you must be prepared to hold your investments for the long haul.

Mutual Funds

These are investment companies run by professional managers who pool the assets of numerous investors and then issue shares. Because you can get in and out of mutual funds at any time at little or no cost, these are terrific vehicles for small investors.

Tax-deferred 401k Plans

Since 401k plans are one of the few government tax shelters around, anyone who does not make the maximum use of these plans is really being foolish. If you are eligible for a 401k plan, invest the maximum amount, because everything in a 401k is tax deferred, which is to say you don't have to pay any capital gains tax or income taxes of any kind. That is where you want your high income as well as your highest appreciation. Unfortunately, surveys show that less than two-thirds of the people eligible to invest in 401k plans actually take advantage of them.

If you work for a corporation or private company, a 401k is a tax-deferred retirement plan that gives you a quick and painless way to save and invest for your retirement. The money comes directly out of your paycheck and goes into the plan. Because many companies have a contribution matching plan, usually kicking in one dollar for every two of yours, the money accumulates fast. After retirement you will have to pay taxes on the money invested in a 401k, but by that time presumably you'll be in a lower tax bracket. In the meantime you've been earning returns on the entire pre-tax amount, which, according to one study, will leave you 54 percent ahead of where you'd have been if you'd paid the taxes up front.

Health Insurance

Everyone needs to make sure that health policies, and catastrophic health policies in particular, are part of their asset plans. Illness is very costly, both in terms of lost working time and the medical expenses themselves. Individual plans, whether offered to groups or your employer (or a previous employer if you are retired) become a necessity. Health insurance is perhaps the most important asset you should have.

Life Insurance

Term life is a very important part of an asset program. Whole life has a very low rate of return, but term life policies are needed for people who haven't yet put aside enough money to take care of their family in the event of their death. Accidents do happen. People get sick, have car accidents, and die before the actuarial averages say that they should. Life insurance is one way to reach your family's financial goals if you aren't there to do it in person. Once you are rich enough, there isn't any real need for life insurance. But since one can never be too rich or too thin, life insurance may always play a part in asset planning.

Real Estate

Real estate offers perhaps the highest returns of all in the long run. But prices are volatile and offer very little in the way of liquidity (easy convertibility into cash). Compared to publicly traded securities, real estate investments tend to be indivisible. If you need cash, you can always sell 10 percent of your stocks. You can't sell two apartments in a twenty-apartment building. Indivisibility and illiquidity are two factors inherent in real estate. Real estate may have a place as a portion of an investment portfolio. But you have to be paid for its illiquidity and indivisibility. And therefore your overall return should be greater.

While real estate may be part of your investment portfolio, your home is not. Your home's location has more to do with your children's education, your safety, convenience, the availability of things like airports and freeways, or the avoidance of them.

Gold

Unlike currencies, gold bullion tends to maintain its purchasing power in times of crisis, thus protecting its owner from disruptions in the world's monetary system. People who bought gold before the crash of 1929 were in far better shape in the years that followed than people who owned only stocks. Traditionally gold prices surge when inflation starts to climb. Double-digit inflation rates during the Carter years pushed gold to $875 an ounce. But lower inflation ever since has pushed gold prices down to $350.

Because there are so many better ways to protect yourself from inflation, many investors now ignore gold entirely, with the result that gold is no higher today than it was in 1990. The Dow, in contrast, went up 135 percent over the same period.

Venture Capital

This is money invested in entrepreneurial start-up companies, especially high-tech ones. Because the potential for losing your money is high, so is the potential profit. If you're a venture capitalist you have to be willing and able to take substantial risks. This is not an investment for the inexperienced or fainthearted.

Index Funds

These are mutual funds that try to match the performance of the Dow or the S&P 500. I don't have any objection to index funds themselves. But I have found that index characteristics don't tend to match the client's needs. Either people need more income than an index fund provides or they can take more risk than is associated with an index fund.

Commodities

My father made a lot of money in real estate but only after he first lost everything in the wheat market in 1934. That's why nobody ever buys commodities in our family. This doesn't mean they aren't a good deal for some people. Rule of Thumb: Buy commodities when there is a surplus. Sell when there are shortages.

The Common Stock Advantage

Although the annual rates of return on stocks are more volatile than other assets, over the long term, stocks still generate the highest total returns. The worst five-year period for stocks since 1945 took place from January 1, 1970, to January 1, 1975. Yet even then, the total returns (income plus price change) were still no worse than minus 2.4 percent. Since the early 1940s, neither the S&P 500 nor its predecessor (the S&P 90) has ever declined more than two years in a row.

Despite common stocks being the most profitable elements in any diversified portfolio, they are also volatile. The thought that they could lose 10, 20, or 30 percent of their assets in less than a month terrifies some people. This, coupled with the pessimistic news we hear every day, makes them think that another 1930s-style depression is a distinct possibility.

It may be a possibility, but in the stock market, as in life, you have to go by the odds. The facts are undeniable. For growth and liquidity, nothing beats the stock market over the long term. If someone had taken $1,000 in 1926 and invested it in long-term government bonds, by 1995 that $1,000 would be worth $34,044. If that person had invested in large stocks, however, and reinvested the dividends, that $1,000 would today be worth $1,113,918.

There are a lot of people who like to predict the end of Western civilization, but none of them make much money. On the other hand, people who invest in the future by buying common stocks will see their assets rise in value an average of over 10 percent a year, just as they have over the last seventy years.

Three Ways to Become a Millionaire

1. *Win a lottery.*

2. *Start with $10 million and then lose 90 percent of it.*

3. *Start young, save $100/month and compound it for fifty years.*

The Power of Compounding

Suppose when you were twenty-two years old and had just graduated from college you took 4 percent of your yearly salary and put it in the stock market. On a starting salary of $25,000, you would be saving $1,000 a year. If your salary went up 5 percent per year and the return on your investment was 10 percent (the long-term average return on common stocks), by the time you reached sixty-five you would be worth a million dollars.

This is with a 10 percent rate of return. If you only got 9 percent over forty-three years, the ending value of your savings would be 20 percent less. The million dollars you had at

Table 3.1 Value of Initial Savings

Variables:
Years to Retirement
Compounded Net Worth
Initial Amount

Constant: Rate of Return—10%

Initial Savings, $(000)s	Years to Retirement			
	10	15	20	25
10	$25.9	$41.8	$67.3	$108.3
20	$51.9	$83.5	$134.5	$216.7
50	$129.7	$208.9	$336.4	$541.7
100	$259.4	$417.7	$672.7	$1,083.5
150	$389.1	$626.6	$1,009.1	$1,625.2
200	$518.7	$835.4	$1,345.5	$2,166.9
300	$778.1	$1,253.2	$2,018.2	$3,250.4
400	$1,037.5	$1,670.9	$2,691.0	$4,333.9
500	$1,296.9	$2,088.6	$3,363.7	$5,417.4
750	$1,945.3	$3,132.9	$5,045.6	$8,126.0
1000	$2,593.7	$4,177.2	$6,727.5	$10,834.7

10 percent would now be only $800,000. Now, look at the chunk of money you have to invest, or have already invested. To estimate what its worth will be when you retire, given a 10 percent rate of return on your investments, see Table 3.1.

If the rate of return were to fall to 7.5 percent, you would end up with $550,000 over forty-three years (from twenty-two to sixty-five). A 10 percent drop in the rate of return would result in a 20 percent drop in ending value of savings. A 25 percent drop in rate of return would result in a 45 percent drop in value of savings. A 50 percent drop in rate of return (from 10 percent to 5 percent) would leave you with $325,000 after forty-three years, a 67 percent drop. But since over the

Table 3.2   Ibbotson Long-term Rates of Return, 1926 to 1995

	Approximate Annual Rate	*Adjusted for Inflation*
Large Stocks	10.4%	7.3%
Small Stocks	12.3%	9.2%
Long-term Corporate Bonds	5.6%	2.5%
Long-term Government Bonds	5.1%	2.0%
Treasury Bills	3.7%	0.6%
Inflation	3.1%	0.0%

SOURCE: Computed using data from *Stocks, Bonds, Bills & Inflation 1996 Yearbook*, Ibbotson Associates, Chicago (annual updates work by Roger G. Ibbotson and Rex Sinquefield). Used with permission. All rights reserved.

last seventy years the stock market has averaged a 10 percent rate of return we can safely count on your being a millionaire.

Now at this point you might say to yourself, "Hey, wait a second. The government already charges me 12 percent for social security. That means that my social security alone should be worth a minimum of $3 million when I retire. So we already have a program in place that should make every American a multimillionaire."

So where are they, America's social security millionaires? Well, there aren't any, which is one reason why I say, if you expect to enjoy a happy, secure old age, you're going to have to do it yourself.

Eighth Wonder of the World

The fact that bonds pay less than stocks and T-bills pay less than bonds doesn't matter much if you are only talking about one or two years. But if you are looking at thirty years, the differences can be dramatic.

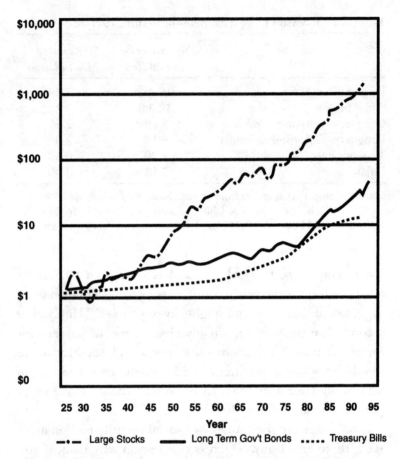

Figure 3.1   *Value of One Dollar Invested in 1925: Assorted Asset Classes, 1926 to 1995*

Even if you had invested in large company stocks on January 1, 1929, you would have received an average annual return of 8.5 percent over the next thirty years. By contrast, you would have earned half as much money in long-term corporate bonds—3.7 percent, and slightly over a third as much in long-term government bonds—2.9 percent, or intermediate government bonds—2.8 percent. Investments in a common cash instrument, ninety-day U.S. Treasury bills, returned 1.0 percent on average, effectively losing money when factoring in inflation.

Over the past thirty years, a similar pattern is evident. The average annual return for small company stocks—10.7 percent—significantly exceeds that for long-term corporate bonds—8.5 percent; long-term government bonds—7.9 percent; intermediate-term government bonds—8.4 percent; and ninety-day treasury bills—6.7 percent.

To paraphrase David Rockefeller, compounding is the eighth wonder of the world. A $10,000 stock investment in 1965 would have been worth $210,118 in 1995, compared with only $115,582 if the money had been put in long-term corporate bonds (see Table 3.2 and Figure 3.1).

When to Invest Yourself and When to Have an Investment Advisor

If you are starting with under $100,000, you probably don't want, can't afford, and don't need an investment advisor. When you are dealing with small amounts of money you get killed on the transaction costs. Minimum commissions are the same whether you are selling one, ten, or 100 shares. If you plan to buy and sell individual securities, the lowest transaction cost is $30 to $40. Schwab is $39. If you sell just one share of stock your transaction cost is still $39 a share.

This is a lot of money per share, especially when the average price per share is only $55 or $60. If you buy just ten shares, the stock has got to go up 10 to 15 percent just to pay the round trip cost on commissions. That's a tough nut to crack.

Even if you do a low turnover strategy (turning over 20 percent of your portfolio every year), that still means you have to make a 2 percent bogie just to break even. If you do a high turnover strategy (turning over 90 percent to 100 percent of your stock every year), the transaction costs are absolutely prohibitive. You may start out with $100,000 and after a giant bull market you still end up with $100,000.

If all you have to invest is $100,000, you're better off in mutual funds than in individual stocks. The whole idea of mutual funds is that they are a joint activity. Instead of just investing $1,000 a month, when you combine your money with that of 1,000 other people each investing $1,000 a month, you get purchasing power and leverage.

One caveat: Be careful not to over-diversify. It is not unusual for people with just $100,000 to own two or three equity funds from each of two or three families of equity funds. They end up putting $5,000 to $10,000 in each fund with some in bonds and some in cash.

This is pure overkill—diversification layered on diversification. If you are just investing $100,000, a couple of equity funds within one family is all you need.

People who have portfolios worth over $1 million, on the other hand, will probably want to invest in individual stocks. If you're good at this and have the time, you may want to handle the investing yourself. Be advised, however—it's not as easy as it looks. Many people who start out trying to do their own investing soon discover they'd rather spend their time doing things they are good at, such as working at their regular profession, and leave their investing to someone who can devote himself to it full time.

While it's pretty clear what to advise people who have less than $100,000 or more than $1 million to invest, it's a lot harder to know what to tell people in the middle. If you go out and hire an investment advisor to manage your $500,000, you may end up short-changed. You may think you are going to get individual management, but, in fact, you are just buying product. People who do this usually end up in a co-mingled vehicle. At that level the firm may lump smaller investors together to lessen the management costs, giving you a real cookie-cutter approach to whatever strategy they employ. What you end up with are individualized securities and some advice in terms of the mix. The Securities and Exchange Commission doesn't like co-mingled vehicles because what you have created in effect is an unregistered mutual fund. But the reality is you have to do that. It is the only thing that is economically feasible.

The Best Mix

When you retire you are going to need more income from your investments to replace your former salary. At the same time you want to take less risk because if the market goes in the tank you don't have time to earn it back. Two precautions: always know your net worth and always know the mix.

Diversification is always important. You are always going to want some cash, some bonds, some stocks. How much you put into cash, how much into bonds, and how much into stock depends on: (1) your knowledge, (2) how much time you want to devote to it.

In our private portfolios for individual clients of Spare, Kaplan, Bischel & Associates, we currently aim for a mix about 45 percent stock, 40 percent fixed income (depending on the interest rate), and 15 percent cash. With a private client there is no single best portfolio. Our oldest client is a woman in her late eighties. Our youngest is a woman in her mid-thirties. They have very different investment horizons, very different cost bases and very different tax situations on any scales.

If you don't have the time, the knowledge, or the inclination to plan your investments carefully, there's nothing wrong with being fairly mechanical about it. The important thing is to put something in every payday—something in stocks, something in bonds. It doesn't mean you have to go out and put everything you own into stocks or bonds all at once. Do some analysis. Get some advice. Are bonds cheap, expensive, or somewhere in the middle? Then act accordingly.

When you get a market decline and an opportunity to add to positions at lower prices, don't chicken out. If you expect to make money through stock appreciation, you have to buy stock when it's cheap.

Above all, don't let the market manage your portfolio.

By that I mean that if in 1982 you were pretty aggressive about your portfolio, you probably had 55 percent stocks, 35 percent bonds, and 10 percent cash. If you haven't adjusted the mix since then, due to the way stocks have appreciated, today you will have over 80 percent in stocks, 17 percent in bonds, and less than 3 percent in cash.

Now if a stock/bonds/cash ratio of 55 percent, 35 percent, and 10 percent was right for you in 1982, make sure you don't have over 80 percent in stocks, 17 percent in bonds, and 3 percent in cash today. Don't just sit there fooling yourself, saying, "Eighty percent is really just about right today," because if the market declines, then you'll find yourself saying, "Well, I guess 75 percent is really about right." Then when it declines again, you'll find yourself saying, "Sixty-five percent stock feels about right."

Rather than sit back and let the market manage your portfolio, you have to take the initiative and figure out what's right for you. Have your circumstances changed recently? Are your liabilities different? Did you just get married or divorced? Your kids are getting older. What plans have you made to pay for their college? One is bright, so he's probably getting a scholarship. The other couldn't care less about academics so he's probably not going to college at all. Who knows?

You have to be comfortable with your portfolio and the only way to do that is to make the decisions yourself. The assets have to meet your particular needs. If the portfolio isn't right for you, then it isn't right, period. But you do have to have a portfolio. You do have to start building. You do have to do it now.

How often do you have to re-balance (adjust the mix) on your portfolio?

A year or every six months ought to be plenty often. You don't have to do it daily. The market goes up. The market goes down. What's the forecast for tomorrow? No one has a clue. It's just noise.

Basically you want to strike a middle position between doing nothing (letting the market manage your portfolio) and micro-managing your portfolio (needlessly changing the mix every few days).

Beware of trying to know too much. The more you know about insignificant short-term trends the less able you are to notice important long-term ones. Ignore day-to-day market fluctuations. They are impossible to predict and they don't mean anything anyway. What happens over the next five, ten, or twenty years is infinitely more important than what happens over the next five, ten, or twenty days.

Also, don't worry about politics. Both parties tend to swap economic positions over time. Both parties can help or hurt the economy. The important thing isn't who is president. It's the policies the president inflicts on the rest of us.

CHAPTER 4

—⁓⁓—

Spare's Cheap-Stock
Strategy

The ability to think long term is a terrific advantage to people who keep their feet on the ground, who are stable, who are not easily swayed. If you don't think about what is happening today, this week, or this quarter, but instead look to see what is happening five years from now, the world looks totally different.

Thinking Long-term

The problem in the short run is that you know too much. If you ask, "What are interest rates going to be tomorrow?," everyone has an opinion. But if you ask, "What are rates going to be like five years from now?," no one has a clue.

Same thing with commodities. If you ask people what are commodity price increases going to be like next year, they may very well guess 15 percent, and may be right. But if you ask what commodity prices are likely to be like five years from

---

Spare's Principles of Economics

- There is no fixed relationship between stocks and the economy.

- Institutional investors are no different from the men in the street, they just have more money.

- Don't dance with elephants: You can never be small enough, smart enough, or fast enough to avoid being trampled by a herd of anything.

- Every time you learn the rules, they change the game.

- Reality is better than investors at the bottom believe. Reality is worse than investors at the top believe.

- Love, hate, and neglect affect your portfolio.

- Good things happen to cheap stocks and bad things happen to expensive ones.

---

now, they won't have any information. They'll have to rely on long-term historic trends, which is to say, they'll be forced to conclude that commodities will do what they've always done over the long term—go up a couple percent on average every year.

It's the same with stocks. Currently (early 1997), stocks are overvalued. Could they get even more overvalued in the next six months?

Sure.

What about the next five years?

Probably not.

That's why I say you have to think long term. It cuts out all the short-term noise and clarifies thinking because it forces you to narrow your thinking to essential items. What is normal? What is sustainable? What's the long-term trend?

In the short term, you always get this wild looping stuff on the market. But in the long term you get return to the average, reversion to the mean. If your portfolio has been earning a lot more than some long-term average in the last three years, then by the law of averages the next three years are likely to be rotten.

Do you know that for a fact?

No.

How likely is it that next year will be rotten?

It's hard to say.

Now, if you want to look out three to five years, the odds are they will be rotten because sooner or later the market always reverts to the mean. That's why I can make predictions for five years out but not for one or two or three—when I'm looking at five years, I have no short-term information to distract me. Thus I have to rely on historic long-term trends.

Not everyone appreciates the wisdom of looking out five years. Occasionally I'll tell someone we have to look five years ahead and he will come back, "Who in the hell knows what's going to happen five years from now? The world might not be here."

"Well, it's been here a long time," I usually tell them. "What the hell is five more years?"

Time is important because it helps clarify things. It allows us to get past the passions of the moment, ignore the restless crowd, and do our thinking independently.

Spare's First Principle of Forecasting:
Always Look Far Enough into the Future
That Short-term Information Is of No Use

My goal as an individual is not just to look ahead five years but to project myself out five years and look back to today.

I focus on five years because that is doable. If you focus on today, you won't be able to concentrate on what is likely to be going on five years from now. You keep thinking this is going to happen and that is going to happen, and the truth is most of what is going on is mainly noise.

I'm not saying it's easy to look ahead. I get distracted by today's crises just like anyone else. But if you can look ahead, you'll immediately get a different perspective.

Look back at what seemed so important two years ago. Or try reading a six-month-old newspaper sometime. All those big glaring headlines, those gripping page one stories, don't mean anything anymore. They're gone, forgotten, literally old news. How important is it to you today that a month ago cattle prices went up or down? What you should be looking at is the long view—five years at least, and if you have the time, twenty years is even better.

Why twenty years?

Well, after the second year of the Kennedy administration, the market essentially didn't change for twenty years (from 1962 to 1982, see Figure 4.1).

Was that unique?

Maybe.

Is it legitimate to forecast a similar twenty-year plateau again?

Who knows? In this business, you are always tricked by noise even when you try to be vigilant. I am tricked every day. My goal is just to be less tricked than the competition. If you

December 1925 to December 1965

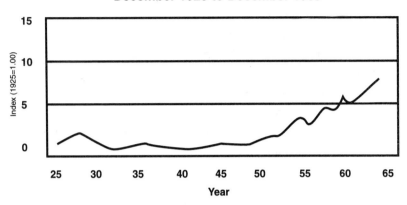

*S&P 90 to 1957; S&P 500 from 1957 to present.

December 1955 to December 1995

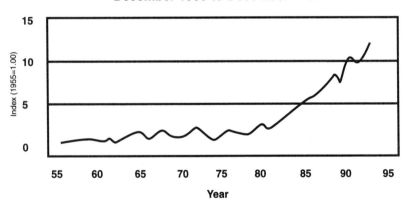

SOURCE: Computed using data from *Stocks, Bonds, Bills & Inflation 1996 Yearbook,* Ibbotson Associates, Chicago (annual updates work by Roger G. Ibbotson and Rex Sinquefield). Used with permission. All rights reserved.

Figure 4.1   *Standard & Poor's 90/500 Price Index, December 1925 to December 1995*

are a day ahead, you win. You don't have to be five years ahead or two years ahead.

In fact, for a professional investment advisor, it can be harmful if you are too far ahead. The stock market was overvalued in 1925. But any investment advisor going around telling that to his clients had no clients by 1926.

Was he right?

Yes. But being an investment advisor isn't a question of being in some absolute scientific sense right or wrong. You just have to be more right than your competitor.

Cheap Stocks and the Contrarian Personality

Some business people are more successful when they're part of a crowd and some people are more successful when they go their own way. In the thirty years I've been an investment advisor, whatever success I've had has been based on going my own way, which is why, when people asked how I got started in this business, I tell them I was a "failed bank trainee."

Whatever skills I might have developed in the Stanford business school, balancing checkbooks for little old ladies wasn't one of them. As soon as I got my MBA, I went to work for the Bank of California. Even then I took the attitude that I never worked for anyone. I *reported* to them. I worked *with* them but I never worked *for* them. One reason I left banking was that the head of loan examinations hauled me off to Modesto to do a loan examination. He wanted me to look at the documentation for the loan and make sure all the assets were there. I said, "No. I wasn't hired to count collateral." The way I saw it I had been hired to look at credit for loans, not waste my time sitting in a bank vault counting certificates and deeds of trust.

Unfortunately he couldn't see the issue from my point of view and when we got back to San Francisco, he tried to have me fired. A fine gentleman by the name of L. Harvey Davis saved my career by plucking me out of branch banking and putting me in the credit department, from which I subsequently moved to the investment department.

The Bank of California didn't have a big investment department in the mid-sixties. But it was growing, and investment management suited my personality, which, according to my performance evaluations, was rather too opinionated and independent anyway. Ironically, those are the very qualities our firm looks for today when trying to hire investment managers—the ability to make up one's own mind, a disinclination to run with the pack, and a lack of concern about what other people think. Eventually the bank figured that they weren't such bad qualities either, because they fired my boss and put me in his place.

Our department made a lot of money for the bank during my tenure there. We had developed a new evaluation technique that allowed us to decide which stocks were cheap (worth more than their price would indicate) by comparing those stocks to the overall state of the market. Unfortunately, the Bank of California seemed more interested in taking the profits from our department and opening new branches than reinvesting it in our highly productive profit center.

In frustration, in the summer of 1989 I got together with a group of investment division employees and together we offered to buy the investment management business from the bank.

They weren't pleased. The Bank of California was owned by Mitsubishi, which was so big our little buyout offer didn't even register on their radar screen. Besides, I don't think they wanted to start a precedent by allowing employees to dictate terms to them. My boss's boss called me into his office and told me, (1) they were rejecting our buyout offer, and (2) I had to decide: Did I want to be a company man or an entrepreneur? "No more negotiations," he told me. "We will give you an employment contract instead."

I had never had an employment contract. So I took it to a labor attorney, who literally started mumbling about "slavery" and "involuntary servitude."

I could see there was no future at the bank on terms I could accept, so I resigned the next day. Over the next couple of days, several other investment division employees resigned as well and on the following Monday we opened up a new firm in rent-a-room offices on Montgomery Street. That was in August 1989. Now our firm, still on Montgomery Street (though in much-improved quarters), has over thirty employees and manages more than $2.5 billion in assets.

Throughout all this our attitude has never changed: we work for ourselves; we do our own thinking; no one tells us what to do. This isn't arrogance. It's the attitude you have to have if you expect to survive and prosper by investing in cheap stocks. I see myself as "a contrarian non-trend follower," which is to say I avoid the herd, the market enthusiasms, the huge mania for one hot stock or another that seems to envelop the market every so often. Early in my career, I learned if you always go where the herd goes and buy what the herd buys it doesn't matter whether you have invested in a great company with a great product in an expanding market or not. When the herd falls in love with a company, it bids up the stock price so high you can't make any money anyway.

On the other hand, when the herd decides to desert a stock for one irrational reason or another, it drives down the price of the stock so low that you can buy it for less than an objective evaluation of company prospects shows it is really worth. In the language of investors, the stock is "cheap." Then when the company gets its act together and corrects whatever problem caused the depressed prices in the first place, other investors will jump in and drive up the stock price. But by this time, you will have taken your profits and will be long gone.

Evolution of a Cheap-Stock Buyer

When I say our company buys cheap stocks, I'm not talking about stocks that sell, for instance, under $10 a share. Cheap, as defined by our company, has nothing to do with a stock's absolute price. Rather it is a synonym for value, for stocks that are inexpensive compared to what they would cost if investors were not so quick to abandon perfectly good stocks from sound companies in growing sectors of the economy just because some company had a bad quarter or two.

I first began to consider the notion of buying cheap stocks back in 1972 when I was assistant director of research for the Bank of California trust department. Although I was only the assistant research director, basically I was running the department.

When you work in a trust department you have to be able to meet the needs of income beneficiaries (typically surviving spouses) at the same time that you also provide for the remainder interests (usually children or grandchildren). When someone who had established a trust with our department (the grantor) died, the usual arrangement was that the surviving spouse (generally the wife) would receive the income from the trust for the rest of her life; when she died the principal would go to the children or grandchildren.

The problem in this kind of situation is that the trust really has two divergent goals. The widow, since she's not going to get the principal anyway, doesn't really care whether the trust grows or not. What concerns her is the income the trust generates.

The children or grandchildren, on the other hand, are not so concerned about income as they are about how much the trust is worth—what do they get in five or ten or twenty years when the trust is dissolved and the funds are distributed?

What the trust department has to do is balance the interests of both parties—manage the trust so as to generate as much income as possible for the widow and at the same time increase the assets to the full extent possible for the next generation. Since it's impossible to maximize income and assets at the same time, the trust department has to look for balance. In fact, the law requires it—one has to consider the interests of both parties equally.

Prior to 1972, our analysis (and indeed the analysis of most bank trust departments) wasn't particularly sophisticated. Usually we invested our trust accounts in well-known, well-regarded Tier One growth stocks (in those days known as the Nifty Fifty). Since growth stocks primarily worked to benefit the children by making the assets grow very fast, in order to meet the needs of the widow we also tossed in some income stocks without much consideration as to whether they were cheap (a good value for the money) or not. The attitude was, "Yeah, mom needs some income, so we'll keep her quiet with a few oil stocks, banks, or electrical utilities."

This worked fine in a bull market, but bull markets are like flowers in the spring—they don't last forever. A mortifying object lesson was headed my way and its name was Polaroid.

Wild About Polaroid

By 1972, I'd been in the investment business seven years. Justifiably or not, I took a lot of pride in what I regarded as my uncanny ability to separate artifacts from information and hype from reality. No person or stock was going to fool me very badly or for very long. Then in October 1972, I met Polaroid's new SX-70 instant color camera and forgot everything I thought I ever knew.

Everyone in the business had known for the previous six months that Polaroid was working on something hot. The announcement was to be made in Miami. I asked my boss for the day off, flew all night from San Francisco, and arrived in Miami at 8 A.M. on a hot, humid morning, all of which detracted not one bit from the excitement surrounding the Polaroid product announcement.

The buzz was unbelievable. This wasn't just another product announcement by just another high-tech company—it was a combination coronation-beatification of Polaroid's founder and head research engineer, Dr. Edwin Land. As soon as you walked in the ballroom, on all sides there was this huge trumpeting—"It's marvelous; it's wonderful; Dr. Land is a true genius; his SX-70 camera is revolutionary."

And it was true. Dr. Land was a genius and his camera was an engineering triumph. On the other hand, that had nothing at all to do with the question I was there to try to answer—was Polaroid a good buy for the investment department of the Bank of California? If the market had already included Dr. Land's genius and his whiz-bang SX-70 camera in the price of the stock, the stock was overpriced and it didn't matter in a sense how great the product might or might not be—for investors at that point the stock was a nonstarter.

A month later, still hot on Polaroid's trail, I snuck into a meeting of optical engineers in San Francisco—I was still young enough to pass myself off as a student—and now there was more noise and more mania all over again. Dr. Land was sitting in a chair on a raised platform, surrounded by floodlights. The optical engineers were even more enthusiastic than his own people had been in Miami. I think it was this more than anything that convinced me that Polaroid had no limit. A lot of people at the San Francisco optical engineer meeting worked for the competitor, Eastman Kodak. And they were out there cheering Dr. Land as hard as any of the Polaroid people: "Land's a genius!" You heard it on all sides.

Well, that sort of thing was hard to resist. It's one thing to hear all this enthusiasm from the company's own employees, but when you hear it from the competition as well, you lose any sense of reality. I went back to my office and told everyone about the terrific reception that Land got. I was so emotional about it, I could hardly talk about the company without getting tears in my eyes. It was very sad. I just totally lost it.

When I first began urging the bank to buy Polaroid, the stock was at about $110. And the higher it went the more enthusiastic I got. (Eventually the Bank of California put about 1 percent of a billion-dollar investment portfolio into Polaroid.) At the peak of the frenzy, the stock was well above $140 per share. But it was wildly overpriced—total market capitalization (outstanding shares times price) was $4.5 billion, but company revenues were only $300 million, with projections to go up to $500 million. The problem was obvious (or it ought to have been obvious to anyone not swept away in the mania)—even with the most bullish revenue projections, Polaroid stock was so expensive on a market-capitalization-to-revenues basis you might not make any money with the stock for the next ten years. And that's assuming that everything went perfectly smoothly.

Of course something did go wrong. Originally the camera was to have been small and lightweight enough to carry in your pocket. The final product was too big and heavy for that. Although the camera was an engineering triumph, it was far from perfect. Even at the announcement, a few people were going around with magnifying glasses pointing out that the resolution wasn't nearly as good as it first appeared. Reds were great; greens were okay; blues were not so hot. And that was the good news.

Polaroid had to invent new facilities for the SX-70. It wasn't just a matter of putting two layers of film together as in the old black and white days. Now they had polymer chemistry between two layers of plastic being squeezed through rollers interacting in just the right sequence. It was a brand-new process in a brand-new camera. A lot of breakthrough thinking went into the SX-70. The camera didn't use normal round batteries. The batteries were flat and were included in the film package instead of going in the camera.

Because Polaroid never expected to make money on the camera, it was counting on film sales to provide the profits. Initially industry analysts had projected that the "burn rate" (number of rolls of film shot) of the average camera buyer would be about five rolls per year. But as it turned out, people were only using one or two.

Over the next six months, the stock dropped from above $140 to $100. Six months later it fell to $50. And three months after that it was down to less than $20. All of a sudden the emperor had no clothes. The bottom fell out. Investors were stunned. We all just sort of sat there saying, "oh, oh, oh," as the stock price spiraled down the tubes.

Although the people in our department were a bit stunned by the plummeting prices, the decision to jump into Polaroid wasn't *entirely* my fault. I used to go to meetings where I would talk about Polaroid and the people who had been through such things before (and thus supposedly knew better than to get swept away by manias) would say, "Gee, Tony, that's really terrific." Not once was I ever questioned.

Not once did anyone ever say, "Gee, are you sure that's true?" It was all just a positive reinforcement—until the stock started to fall.

Despite my spectacular misjudgment here, the collapse of Polaroid wasn't the total disaster it might have been. The amounts of money invested were not huge when considering the overall size of the portfolio. And I was hardly the only analyst—either in the Bank of California or anywhere else— who had gotten swept away by growth stock mania. Analysts weren't just gaga over Polaroid, they were also wild about Coca Cola, Procter & Gamble, Eastman Kodak, Avon, and IBM. Avon was $130. Then in the bear market of 1973–74, it dropped all the way to $10. A similar drop hit IBM. So there was nothing unique about Polaroid. It looked no different than forty or sixty other growth stocks. They all were over-priced and everyone who bought them got his head handed to him on a platter.

Despite all this I was grateful for the experience. For me it was like going to graduate school at Polaroid. The most valuable lesson I learned was that value really does count. You can't get swept away by the noise. If the price of a stock is based on mania, then you have to forget it. You can't just tell yourself the company's product is so great there's no way an investment can fail. Given the price of Polaroid's stock, there was no way our investment could succeed.

The funny thing was, there never came a time when I was discouraged about Polaroid. I thought it was terrific when it peaked above $140. We pulled the plug when it got to $60. When the stock finally bottomed out at $14, I was *still* pushing it, this time on the grounds that now it was "really cheap." Although at this point I was finally right about the stock, no one was interested anymore—"Polaroid? God, Spare, not Polaroid!"

Origins of the Cheap Stock Strategy

One good thing came out of the crash of Polaroid, Avon, and the rest of the Nifty Fifty in the 1973–74 bear market—it forced us to rethink our investment strategy (or what passed for our investment strategy) for our trust accounts. "We have to find a better way," we said. "We have to find some classes of assets that simultaneously help both the income beneficiary and the remainder interests."

At the time there was an investment strategist at Donaldson, Lufkin & Jenrette securities corporation named Ted Shen who used to publish books of graphs on a wide variety of relative relationships. One of these graphs showed "relative yield"—the dividend yield of a given stock divided by the market's overall yield. (Dividends are a share of the profits voted by a company's board of directors. Yield is the ratio of the dividend to the stock price.) Suddenly a light went on over my head. This was exactly what the trust department had been looking for!

Stocks that had high dividend yields when compared to the dividend yield of the S&P 500 would provide high incomes for our trusts' income beneficiaries. At the same time, because these stocks were also cheap (that was one of the things that made their yields so high), they also had potential for high growth, thus satisfying the need for asset appreciation for the remainder interests.

We started using this evaluation technique, which we subsequently named Relative Dividend Yield (RDY), in January of 1975 to help pick stocks for our trust accounts. Later we went to institutional investors such as endowment funds, foundation funds, and pension plans, showed them the results, and began using it as the basis for their investments as well. We've been doing it ever since.

Using Relative Dividend Yield

The RDY approach, by comparing the yield of a given stock with the yield of the S&P 500 (published weekly in Barron's), allows you to determine when stocks are out of favor and therefore cheap. It doesn't rely on predictions or earnings. It has nothing to do with trend following or momentum. Instead it determines which stocks are cheap without any clue as to whether they are going to do well next week, next month, next quarter, or even next year. It looks at whether a stock is cheap on a three-, four-, or five-year basis, and in the meantime you get an income stream to live on. Or as we cheap stock enthusiasts like to say, "You get paid to be patient."

Although we have found RDY to be highly reliable where it works, it only applies to certain kinds of stocks—big companies with an above-market yield. It doesn't work for small companies, companies with below-market yields, or companies that don't issue dividends. RDY works best when the market is weak and worst when it is strong. Although RDY still gives you an above-average rate of return over the longer term, where it really out-performs other strategies is in a flat or bear market.

Generally, when using RDY we like to get a minimum of 125 percent of market yield (a stock's yield divided by the S&P 500's yield should equal 1.25 or greater). Some stocks are very unattractive at the same level that other stocks are attractive. An electrical utility isn't attractive until it's at 180 percent to 200 percent of market yield, and if it falls below a 60 percent premium we sell. On the other hand, if we can buy a fallen angel growth stock like Eastman Kodak 40 percent to 50 percent above market yield, we consider that a good deal.

Although the RDY technique is really a very radical approach, it only really works on a portion of perhaps the 900 largest securities. Because it focuses on dividends, it also only works in countries like the United States, where there is a dividend commitment culture. Unlike foreign companies, American companies tend to see dividends as a proportion of normal sustainable earning power. They assign internal staff people to work on them. They have external investment bankers looking at them. Thus when an American company sets its dividend, it has to be taken seriously because it represents the company's own best estimate of its prospects. (For a detailed explanation of the RDY approach, see *Relative Dividend Yield,* by Anthony Spare with Nancy Tengler, John Wiley & Sons, 1992.)

Market-Capitalization-to-Revenues Ratio

An approach with much wider applicability is market-capitalization-to-revenues ratio. Market cap is figured by multiplying a stock's price by the number of outstanding shares. To get market-cap-to-revenues, you then divide market cap by sales (revenues). Expensive stocks have high market-cap-to-revenues ratios (six or eight). With cheap stocks, the market cap may be close to one or even lower.

One problem with market-cap-to-revenues is that it varies with the size of a company and is different from industry to industry. If a company is growing, its market cap will vary over time. Retail companies, for instance, tend to have very low market-cap-to-revenues. Similarly sized drug companies, on the other hand, have always had high ones (see Figure 4.2).

Unlike RDY, the market-cap-to-revenues strategy works with any size company, not just large ones, applies equally well to foreign and domestic companies, and isn't limited to

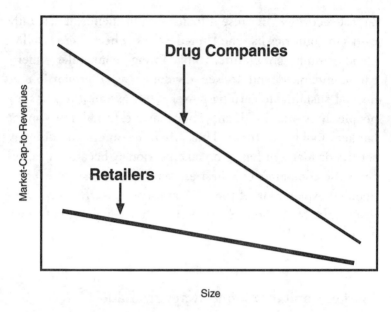

Figure 4.2   *Market-Cap-to-Revenues Versus Company Size, in Two Selected Industries*

companies with above-market yields. On the other hand, it isn't as reliable overall and doesn't give you that clean winning relationship you get with RDY. As a result, whenever we can, we use both of them together. Sometimes we identify pharmaceutical companies as cheap using RDY, and then we use the market-cap-to-revenue technique as a backup. Even if a company has a high RDY, you want to make sure it isn't selling at an outrageously high market-cap-to-revenue figure. One way to do that is to look at the history of the company in question. As companies get bigger, the relationship of their market-cap-to-revenues declines. A $2 billion market cap company is going to sell at a lower ratio on average than a $10 billion company. Microsoft, at the same multiple of revenues, is more expensive today than it was ten years ago.

When using RDY on a small company, on the other hand, a high yield means little. Perhaps the company made a mistake and set the dividend too high. Because small companies have more trouble borrowing money, they can't keep dividends up during a bad quarter. A banker will tell the company, "I'm not going to lend you money. You've got problems." Large companies, on the other hand, have no trouble getting money from banks and thus find it easier to pay dividends despite a bad quarter.

Good-bye to Glamour

If you use RDY and market-cap-to-revenues to pick your stocks, you will most likely end up with a rewarding and profitable portfolio, but it won't be an especially glamorous one. When you invest in cheap stocks, you don't end up with Microsoft or Netscape or any high-tech glamour stocks featuring moon rocks, ruby lasers, or cancer cures. In fact your stocks may not do anything for the next quarter or even the next year. But if you are willing to wait because you know the stock is basically a good value, eventually it will go up. And when it does, everyone else suddenly will recognize it too. Then once the price begins to soar, you cash in your chips, get off the ride, and go looking for another cheap stock with which to start the process all over again.

———⟋⟋⟋⟋———

CHAPTER 5

The Art of
Picking Cheap Stocks

Despite techniques like RDY and market-capitalization-to-revenues ratios, there's no infallible way to tell whether a stock is cheap or not. RDY and market-cap are rough guides, not precision tools. They help you close in around a stock's true value in broad bands. Is a stock: (1) cheap, (2) fair valued, or (3) expensive? And for our purposes, that's good enough—we would always rather be roughly right than precisely wrong.

Heavy quantitative analysis doesn't work when you're doing a value approach. Anyone who is using that kind of massive machinery is looking in the wrong place because, unless he focuses on the interrelationship of yield, yield change, and long-term time horizons, he won't pick up what we do.

I also don't think you can find cheap stocks by looking at earnings. Market-capitalization-to-revenues gives you better information, but again, there is no mechanical number. It changes as the company grows and is different in different industries. Retailing, for example, has always sold at a very low market-cap-to-revenue. The drug industry has always sold at a very high market-cap. A large company will have a different market-cap-to-revenues than the same company did when it was small.

The Cost of Information

The cost of information is not free. When you hear good (or bad) things about a company, so does everyone else. What is known about a stock gets reflected in the price. You can't rely on financial reporters to tell you what to do. They don't have the same goals. A good reporter will tell you, "Here are the five reasons not to own XYZ company."

As a cheap stock investor, you don't care about any of that. All you want to know is whether those reasons are reflected in the price. If they are, you say, "Okay, I know those five reasons and at $20 a share everyone else does too. The stock is cheap. It's time to buy."

Suddenly the stock goes to $40 and now all the financial reporters are saying, "Here are the five good reasons to own XYZ." There is nothing wrong with their reasons. They just aren't part of the investor's decision-making process. The cheap stock investor sits there and says, "This is terrific. I know those five great reasons to own this stock. But at $40, they are already in the price. I can't make any money."

Don't get spooked just because some stock you've been watching suddenly drops far lower than you expected. Most companies, I've found, are far more stable than investor attitudes about the company. Most investors get so spooked by shadows they end up making a stock more volatile than the company's prospects really warrant.

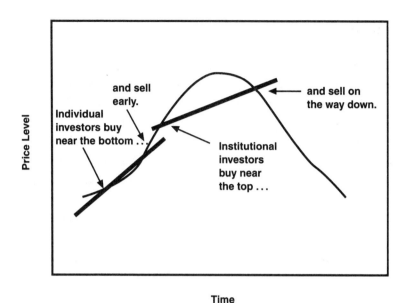

Figure 5.1 *Why Individuals Do Better Than Institutions*

As a cheap stock investor, you may hear criticism that cheap stock investors such as yourself tend to sell too soon. And that may be true. But when does an institution typically buy and sell?

Oftentimes institutions buy when a stock is near the peak and sell when the stock is on the way down, which is one reason why they typically make less money than individual investors while taking more risk. Individual investors, on the other hand, consistently take less risk and make more money (see Figure 5.1). On a total return (dividends plus appreciation), that's particularly true because individuals with high yield stocks can sit there and say, "Well at least I'm getting an income. I'm getting paid to be patient."

Safety Through Diversity

Unlike many investors in growth stocks, cheap stock investors tend to have reasonable expectations about total return. If they're getting 3.5 percent, 4.5 percent, or 6 percent current returns on income they're happy. They say, "That's fine—that's about what I get in a savings account. But this way I get to own a common stock that could very well appreciate." So they hold on to the stock. They learn patience and discipline and they collect dividends in the meantime.

Now you might argue that there's a good reason that their cheap stock investments are cheap—the company's in trouble and it's headed for the toilet, where there won't be any dividends at all.

Well, you could be right. And that's exactly the reason you want a diversified portfolio. If you own two or three electrical utilities, for instance, what are the chances that the boards of directors of all three companies are going to cut dividends simultaneously?

It's remote. We make the odds remoter still by taking a very conservative approach. Out of the perhaps sixty or seventy stocks we own at Spare, Kaplan, Bischel & Associates at any one time, we have perhaps ten or twelve utilities, each diversified by fuel source (gas, oil, coal, nuclear), economic sector, and regulatory commission. This way, whatever affects one utility most likely won't affect any of the others.

We also protect our investors by eliminating very high market-capitalization-to-revenues stocks. If a company went from ten times revenues to five times, it is still expensive and the fact that it is much lower than four years ago really doesn't impress us.

The Case Against Earnings

A lot of investors think earnings are very important. We don't. We don't look at earnings—not trailing 12-month earnings, price-to-earnings ratios (PEs), or forecasted earnings. And the reason is that they don't predict anything. If the idea is to do well—to avoid selling at the bottom and buying at the top— PEs don't help you.

Now a lot of people don't agree with this. They look and see what the PE (also called the multiple) is for the market. And if the market is at 14.5 times earnings and the PE for a given stock is less than that, then they say, "Well, it's lower. The stock isn't overpriced. It's okay to buy."

To me, the PE is an empty number. It doesn't tell you anything. Maybe the reason PEs are low is that earnings are too high. You can't evaluate a stock mechanically. It's as much an art as anything else. You have to look at everything. It's like mathematician and songwriter Tom Lehrer used to say, "Don't shade your eyes—plagiarize." Take a bit from here, a piece from there, put together a collage that seems to make sense, and for Godsakes, have a long enough time frame. Don't try to outguess tomorrow, next week, next month, next quarter. No one ever made any money thinking that way. Do what is doable, not what no one else has ever done before.

Throwing Out the Price-to-Earnings Ratio

If you are a cheap stock buyer, the one thing you don't want to be doing is trying to time the purchase of stocks, and if you are a trend follower/extrapolator/trader, the one thing you don't want to do is face a bad quarter. If you don't believe in the market because you think it's overvalued, you don't want to take any chances. At the tail end of bull markets, the market bobbles around a lot. If you're a speculator and you don't have any conviction, what do you play?

Well, you tend to play what is popular because you know it's a short-end game.

Consider the example of Microsoft, which in January 1997 hit $100 a share (shortly after the company executed a two-for-one split). If Microsoft had had just one sneeze indicating that their next quarter wasn't going to meet expectations, the stock wouldn't have been 100 before the split—it would have been 50 or lower.

Well, if you came into the game thinking, "Microsoft is only worth $25 a share," you don't own it. People who do own Microsoft do so because they have convinced themselves that it is not going to fall to 50, that it is not going to fall to 30, that it isn't even going to have a bad quarter. They sit there and tell themselves, "The stock has momentum and they aren't even going to talk about quarterly earnings for another couple of weeks." Then two weeks go by and nothing has happened so they say to themselves, "Maybe I got another two weeks."

This is a very dangerous tail-end game. When you see prices go up for no reason, watch out. It isn't normal. Bad things are about to happen.

If Microsoft were to fall to 30, it would be a good deal but no one would want to buy it, especially institutions.

Why?

Because most institutions don't buy stocks in decline. Companies whose stocks are headed down have earnings problems. The market will say, "We have a problem with management credibility." And you will get every ridiculous reason under the sun for not buying the stock when it is down and low and cheap.

That's a hard way to make money. People who think perfectly clearly in all other respects will rationalize anything when it comes to the stock market. It cannot be that the market was a better value at 6,700 than it was at 1,000 and yet people will do anything to justify their buying in an expensive market, including looking at such meaningless numbers as price-earnings ratios.

Now what was the PE when the Dow was 1000?

Twenty-seven.

What was the PE in early 1997?

Eighteen.

Do you really think the market *was* cheaper at 18 than it was at 27?

If you don't, you really should just throw out the PEs and pay no attention to them because they're obviously giving you bad information. The market cannot be cheaper at 6,700 than it was at 1,000. It cannot be!

Then you say, "Well, maybe the market isn't really expensive today. Maybe it was just incredibly cheap at 1,000 and now it's fairly valued."

Maybe.

But it is not cheaper than it was. And yet there are people out there saying, "Hey, look at the PE—it's only 18! What a great time to buy."

Why Revenues Matter (and Earnings Don't)

When we buy a stock at Spare, Kaplan, Bischel & Associates, the first thing we want to look at is market yield. If the stock is below market yield, we use market-cap-to-revenues. If the yield is above market, we use RDY and we also take a peek at market-cap-to-revenues. We don't look at PEs. Earnings play no part in evaluation techniques such as yield, yield change, market-cap-to-revenues, and price-to-book (market price of a stock divided by shareholders' equity per share). The reason is we simply don't trust earnings. They can't be forecasted—not by analysts, accountants, or anyone else. Not only don't most companies know what next year's earnings are going to be, they don't even know what last year's earnings were. That is why you get revisions in which operating earnings suddenly become nonoperating earnings.

Now it's true there are always some companies at which the management thinks it can fake investors out and it's right—it can, for the short run. Eventually, though, investors catch on.

That's another reason to be looking at market-cap-to-revenues instead of price-to-earnings ratios. You can't do any hocus-pocus with revenues, except fool around a bit with revenue recognition. This is when you pretend you sold something but you really didn't. The revenues are "recognized," but there's no money—only an entry in the receivables column.

I remember a time when some clown down in Silicon Valley faked selling a bunch of computers, had them shipped to a public storage warehouse, collected his commission, and quickly fled town. In another case fifteen years ago, one fellow who worked for a computer company started putting bricks in boxes and passing them off as hard drives. The auditors would come through, pick up the boxes, and think they were looking at hard drives. This made quite a splash in computer circles.

My point is not that people can't cook the books or fool auditors, but that such things are so rare that when they happen they are big news in the industry. This is why you can trust market-cap-to-revenues. It's too hard to fool around with revenues. You can't fake the number of outstanding shares. And the market price is simply the market price—they print it in the paper every day.

Tubesville Forever (or Why Earnings Don't Matter, II)

When you buy cheap stocks, which is to say, stocks that are unloved, rejected, and deserted by the herd for having had a bad quarter or two, the question of the company's management competence immediately arises. Why would anyone, critics ask, want to buy a company that was so badly managed that its stock price collapsed?

Well, as I've said before, companies are never so well managed as investors seem to think when they rush to buy them and drive up the prices out of sight, and they are never so poorly managed as investors clearly believe they are when investors abandon them in droves and send the stock price down the tubes.

This isn't to say there aren't some companies that are clearly better managed than others. Hewlett-Packard, Motorola, Caterpillar, Procter & Gamble, and General Electric have a long history of being well-managed and the trend is likely to continue.

Many investors, however, have a quite different attitude. They think management is brilliant when the company is doing well and terrible when the company is not. What they don't realize is that in most cases they're talking about the same people—the management hasn't changed.

I discovered this good-management/bad-management nonsense back in the mid-sixties when I followed the airline industry. In those days the airlines were still run by former

World War II pilots. The industry was incredibly cyclical. After each cycle, airlines would say, "This time we learned our lesson. We're not going to add excess capacity to our fleets." But then the good times came along and they went out and did it anyway.

After hearing these kinds of excuses three or four times, we finally came to the conclusion that this was just the nature of the business. The operating and financial leverage in airlines is huge. I mean talk about a double bite and a double dip—airlines are a great industry for that. And every time profits soared, airline management was said to be brilliant. And every time profits tanked, the management was denounced as a bunch of idiots. And what was so ironic was that the critics were talking about the same people. Management never changed—only investor attitudes toward them.

If you sit there and say, "Okay, most companies are the best managed when the stock prices are highest and worst managed when the stock prices are lowest," you're really not saying much. What's good management is very subjective. I would much rather deal with value.

Okay, you might say, how do you distinguish between a stock that is cheap and therefore a good buy, and one that is just headed for the tank?

Oftentimes you can't, and this is in spite of in-depth research. This is one of the important differences between running a portfolio and just owning a bunch of stocks. If you are a cheap-stock buyer as we are, every stock we buy is regarded by the herd as tubesville forever. Now the reality is that only maybe one out of forty cheap stocks goes into the tank. And that's what makes it hard—when you have two seemingly identical stocks, both depressed in price, both losing market share, how do you figure out which one will survive and prosper and which one will declare bankruptcy?

How do you decide which one is merely undervalued (irrationally unappreciated by investors) and which one is fundamentally unhealthy (headed straight for the toilet)?

Some signs are obvious. One company has new products, new marketing, new facilities, and the other doesn't. Others are more subtle. How, for instance, do you distinguish between a company merely suffering from excess inventory, and one ailing fatally from an ill-advised acquisition?

In deciding which company will survive you can't go by earnings alone because at the tail end of an advance, the company that's headed for the toilet may very well look like it's doing better because it isn't spending money for the next cycle, investing in new facilities, or coming out with new products. Secondary companies tend to get increases in sales at peaks because the better companies are managed to their level of base growth and not to some short, wild sales spurt.

There used to be a company here in Northern California that competed with Hewlett-Packard in making test and measurement instruments. Most of the time this company ran a distant second to Hewlett-Packard because HP was always so well managed. HP always took the position that it wanted to be running at 100 percent of capacity *at its basic long-term growth rate,* not at the peak demand rate. Although this was a sound strategy, it also meant there eventually would come a time in the last three months, six months, or year of an economic cycle when Hewlett-Packard would flat run out of capacity.

Who had the capacity?

The competition. Hewlett-Packard's main competitor had been running way below capacity. Now all of a sudden if you needed a new instrument, the only place you could get one at the margin was from the competition. They had lower profitability on average because they had much lower market share. But the incremental profit of this new revenue was terrific. Pricing was no problem. In times of high demand, you could name your own price since Hewlett-Packard was sold out.

For the competitor it was a pure windfall. Their volume was going up, prices were increasing, their revenues went through the roof. Since expenses were more or less fixed, earnings were out of sight—until demand started to decline and exposed the company's fundamental weakness: people really preferred Hewlett-Packard instruments. They were better made and better serviced. So when growth in the market went from say, 10 percent a year to merely 5 percent, the competitor's revenues went from plus 15 percent to minus 5 percent.

In the meantime, Hewlett-Packard's revenues continued going up, even during the slowdown, at perhaps 5 percent a year. Hewlett-Packard didn't have terrific profits because it was subject to pricing pressures with much slower than normal growth. In addition, HP was preparing for the next cycle by continuing to spend money on product development, marketing, sales, and its service staff.

But when the market went up again, HP was ready. Every year they added capacity at their long-term growth rate. They had new products. Now suddenly R&D as a percentage of revenues went down. Marketing costs as a percentage of revenue went down.

What went up?

Profits.

There's another reason earnings can be deceptive. Big companies like Hewlett-Packard, General Electric, or Motorola don't like it when their profits go up too fast. They like to show investors a stable growth. Instead of having two years in a row where profits go up 30 percent a year, followed by two years of flat profits, they would much rather have four 15 percent years.

Occasionally they will get surprised. Revenues come in better than budget and expenses remain low. But since they are never quite sure the revenue is there or not, both on the upside and downside they tend to maintain the expense levels. When revenues are worse, good companies don't cut back a lot. The bad companies are forced to.

Why do the better companies prosper?

Well, for one reason, they can get bank financing. Any bank officer would much rather lend money to Hewlett-Packard than some struggling competitor. Just because for a short time Hewlett-Packard's competition had all sorts of zoomy earnings doesn't mean that it ever was the better-run company. This is why I say you can't trust earnings.

—*∿∿∿*—

CHAPTER 6

———◦◦◦———

Disregarding Noise,
Understanding Time

A^t our firm, most of what we tell our clients can be boiled
down to one sentence: Buy cheap stocks and sell expensive
ones. However, that isn't the way the world works. When the
customer calls with questions about the current stock market
buzz, we're expected to have answers.

Dispensing Mumbo Jumbo
When the Real Problem Is Noise

The trick for an individual investor is to know what questions
to ask. For an institutional investor, such as myself, the trick
is to know how much information to throw away as garbage. I
keep track of a lot of stuff because the clients expect it, but
when it comes to making investment decisions, I pay no
attention to most of it.

Short-term traders are forever trying to figure if there is
any information in short-term price changes. Well, there isn't.

No one has ever done a study that can predict the market in the short term. Price change seems to be totally independent one day to the next.

This isn't to say that people don't come up with formulas. Someone looks at what the market did last week or last quarter and devises an empirical formula that explains the changes. The problem is that such formulas invariably fail when one tries to look ahead. There simply is no history of anybody being able to say, "Here are the rules to make successful predictions for tomorrow or next week or next quarter." We might as well take a binary metallic decision maker out of our pockets (a coin) and flip it instead. ·

The fact that there is no way to know what is going to happen in the short term still doesn't prevent people from asking investment advisors whether the market is going up or down tomorrow, next week, or next month. The trick is to be smart enough to know not to answer, and unfortunately I'm never quite that smart. I'll usually throw in something like, "Who knows? It's all noise. There's no way to tell." Then I'll go ahead and give an answer anyway, which proves I'm really dumb.

The truth is, I don't really have any idea why markets vibrate so much—up one day, down the next, and everywhere else in between. If you want the simple answer to what is going on in the market, it's either that there are more investors anxious to sell than buyers anxious to buy and that makes the market go down, or investors are more interested in buying than sellers are in selling and that makes it go up. As to why there might be more buyers one day and more sellers the next, that gets into human psychology. A lot of it I think is pure gamesmanship.

If you buy cheap stocks, over time you will win. If you buy expensive stocks, over time you will lose. Does that mean that every day, every week, every quarter, cheapness always wins? No. Does it mean that expensiveness always loses? No.

Most of what is viewed as business news or financial news is really only news because people need to make a living. If you are really cynical, then you say the news organizations are only providing what human beings crave: certainty, a reason, a rationale for what they see going on in the market but don't understand. If people like me didn't listen to financial news, there wouldn't be financial news. I happily watch *Wall Street Week* and *Nightly Business Review* on TV. I start out every day watching CNBC at 5:30 in the morning. I watch these shows because they are interesting entertainment, but that is what they are—entertainment. I love the *McLaughlin Group*. Oh, I learn something sometimes, but not often.

If people want reasons why the market went up, or if they want to say, "Now I know and understand," that's fine. It doesn't hurt anything—as long as they understand that daily market fluctuations (what I call noise) have less to do with what the Federal Reserve did or what's on the nightly news than with the frenzied trading of institutional investors trying to improve their positions by a tenth of a point.

Bad Stats and Medical Disasters

One of the things that makes the investment business so complicated is that it isn't math; it isn't physics; it isn't Newton's laws. In short, it's not rigorous. Anything that is the sum of psychology, sociology, and economics can't be. This is not a political statement—it's a statistical statement. It's the difference between causality and correlation. It is the difference between understanding and data mining. One of the real problems in today's world is that everyone has huge data files and very quick models, and they can find relationships and build models quickly. On the other hand, if you ask these same people, "Why does it work?" they can't tell you. All they can say is, "It works."

Every model based on past weightings and past relationships falls apart when you try to use it to look ahead. Back in the mid-sixties, someone did a report on General Foods, which at the time was big in coffee. The analyst argued that at age eighteen everyone quits drinking soft drinks and starts drinking coffee. Since there was a huge population bulge that was on the verge of turning eighteen, it was his contention that coffee sales were about to go through the roof. It was nonsense. People didn't suddenly quit drinking Pepsi or Coca-Cola just because they turned eighteen years old. This was just blind faith in historic fact.

Right now you have a bunch of demographers out there arguing that in the second quarter of 1997 we will have a recession because the baby boomer peak will have passed and no one will be buying cars anymore. That's sheer nonsense. Now, this isn't to say that there won't be a recession, but if there is, it won't be because baby boomers aren't buying cars.

This will hardly bother the statisticians. If they can't find a correlation with one phenomenon, they can always find a correlation with something else. Right now a lot of people die of cancer, and as a result, all these researchers out there are furiously looking at the air, the water, environmental toxins, chemicals in rugs, fumes in paint, insecticides on apples, mercury in fish, and all the things we eat. Then they run their correlations and find that water causes cancer, barbecuing causes cancer, dust particles cause cancer, eating apples or fish (and saccharine and MSG and red meat) causes cancer.

Are we really living in an all-pervasive, cancer-causing soup? Of course not. The only reason the cancer death rate is up is that in the past no one lived long enough to die of some of these diseases. All these minute pollutants and toxins they keep finding in the air and water have always been there. It's just that now the techniques for discovering minute amounts of things are so much better. In the past, the equipment could only measure perhaps one part in ten thousand, so we couldn't detect the presence of many of these items. Now the new technology picks up one part in a billion.

False correlations have always existed in economic data too, but before computers, no one knew they were there. Now, with big, fast computers and ever more powerful programs, researchers can generate false correlations so fast it makes your head spin.

If you listen to supply-side guru Jude Wanniski, the reason that government numbers are as bad as they are is that all the original thinking on the subject was done during the thirties, looking back over the previous thirty, fifty, or one hundred years when government spending was small, debt was small, tax rates were small, and the United States enjoyed a laissez-faire economy. For those reasons, Wanniski concluded that all government data had to be faulty just on a theoretical basis. Because we have computers we sometimes think we can turn out better and better information. Oftentimes, they just allow us to turn out bad information faster; other times, they blind us to the facts altogether.

Here's an example. Six years ago, my younger sister passed away. I defy anyone to look at her medical records and figure out why. She was a horse trainer and regularly fell off horses, twice breaking her back, but that wasn't what killed her. She died of a disease called scleroderma. This is one of those really insidious diseases. It doesn't seem to be genetic, but nobody knows what causes it. Doctors think it might be a virus related to one of the T-cell diseases. It randomly attacks organs and makes the joints swell. By the time the symptoms appear, the virus is gone.

We think my sister caught the disease at an Olympic jumping competition in Palm Beach, Florida. She came home sick. Her muscles atrophied, her joints swelled, and she couldn't move. Then the disease attacked her kidneys.

Her youngest daughter offered one of her kidneys for a transplant. The operation was successful—for 24 hours. Then my sister went into septic shock. She lost her kidneys a second time, including her youngest daughter's kidney. The monitors in the hospital went off—her heart stopped—and within a few minutes she was brain dead.

As far as the hospital records are concerned, she died of kidney failure. But what really happened was that the scleroderma caused the kidney failure, which led to septic shock, short-circuiting a successful transplant and causing a heart attack. The records all say that the nurses were there within three minutes, but every nurse knows that if you take longer than that to respond to a heart monitor, the hospital is looking at a big liability case. So no matter how long it really took, they still write down "three minutes."

In short, the records were useless. The underlying cause of her death was scleroderma, but the records all show kidney failure. Five years from now, some Ph.D. is going to sift through all the data and discover a previously unknown correlation between kidney failure and riding horses and publish it in a medical journal. The media will trumpet it as a hitherto unsuspected risk factor. Congress or OSHA or the FDA will come out with a new regulation requiring kidney warning labels on saddles, and a bunch of lawyers will get rich suing horse breeders for selling animals that can cause kidney damage.

As absurd as that sounds, it's no more absurd than hundreds of other supposed correlations found by other Ph.D.s routinely sifting through the nation's data banks. In the fall of 1990 during the Bush administration, Congress decided there was going to be a tax surcharge on luxury cars starting the following January 1. For obvious reasons, luxury automobile sales soared in December and crashed in January. Everyone who had been planning to buy a luxury car in January, February, or March hurried up and made their purchases in December.

Five years from now, a doctoral candidate is going to look at the statistics and conclude that people throughout the country were suddenly overcome with a sudden satiation of desire for luxury automobiles at a time when other Americans were hurting—or whatever sociological claptrap they want to come up with to explain why the luxury automobile market collapsed. In the meantime, they will totally ignore the way taxes distort the economy.

I have a brother-in-law who teaches literature at a college up in Vermont and who understands so little about economics that if you ever asked him if he paid taxes he'd tell you no and sincerely think he was telling the truth. He thinks that because he never has to write a check to the government on April 15 he doesn't really pay taxes. Anyway, that's what he thought until he landed a summer job a few years ago, teaching at a local prison.

At the time, he thought he had hit the jackpot ($300 per week for six weeks)—until he figured out his taxes. His wife also had income from a bookstore. It was the first time he ever understood what their joint marginal effective tax rate was. He was very indignant: "What's this country coming to? It's not worth it to work."

The worst part is, this is not unusual for many Americans. They know what their paycheck is because that's how much they take home. They know what their gross is because they like to compare themselves to everyone else. What people really don't do is make a connection between the two. Few people calculate what their tax rate is, which is unfortunate since, for many of us, taxes are going to make the difference between a happy, comfortable retirement and one full of fear that we can't pay our bills.

Frenzied Trading and Feverish Noise

A lot of people blame the messenger for the fact that the market bounces around so much. But you have to remember: the media is the media. When it comes to what drives the economy, the heads on television are as uninformed today as they were thirty years ago. They think they need to have a rational explanation for every up or down tick in the market. They don't understand that noise is not a relationship. One day they say the market went down because investors feared the Fed was going to cool the economy by tightening interest rates. The next day they say the market went up because the rise in interest rates reduced the danger of inflation, thus giving investors renewed confidence.

It sounds so reasonable, yet it's all nonsense. The Federal Reserve is probably only a follower anyway. When you study economic policy, you discover that what the Fed does today doesn't have an impact for eighteen months—if it has an impact, and even that is questionable to me. In the short run, the cause of market fluctuations is unknowable. It's meaningless noise, most of which, I think, comes simply from having too much irrelevant information.

Someone says, "You know, I think we need up-to-the-minute, live quotes on the Brazilian cruzeiro." Guess what? The Michael Bloomberg data service will say, "Okay, if that is what you want, we'll figure out how to get it."

Bloomberg got his start providing Merrill Lynch bond quotes. Then he went to stocks and eventually to full financial information, company reports, and even baseball scores. Now you can find more on the Bloomberg service than you probably need to know.

So just how helpful is all this information? Most of the time, an individual investor is better off not having it all on hand, especially if he or she is in the market for the long-term. Having information dumped on you by the truckload doesn't give you any advantage. Numbers and facts have never been the secret anyway. It is what you do with the numbers and facts that counts.

When radio, TV, beepers, cell phones, computers, and the Internet put more and more data (most of which is irrelevant) in more and more people's hands in shorter and less meaningful time frames, they only make it harder to siphon off the useful data from the noise. If you think noise is a reason to do something, you're just spinning your wheels. The only way to think clearly about the market is to think long term—three to five years, ten years, or twenty years. You can't pay attention to blips. You have to pay attention to real essences.

Of course, when individual investors do think long term, they get dinged by institutional (professional) investors who claim they don't follow the market; they don't know what they're doing; and as soon as the market starts to go up they dump their stock.

It may be true that individual investors sell too soon, but the reason they can sell early is that they understand long-term value a lot better than institutions, which is why they buy at market bottoms. When you buy at the bottom, it doesn't matter when you sell, because no matter when it is you still make money. Institutional investors, on the other hand, are so fixated on growth stocks that they buy after the bottom is long gone, hold on to stocks through their peaks, and then finally sell when the stock is headed back down.

Professional portfolio managers compound their problems by buying and selling far more frequently than individual investors (the turnover rate for most professionals is 90 percent to 100 percent a year; an individual investor with a long-range strategy, on the other hand, may turn over as little as 20 percent a year). By buying and selling so much, institutional investors get lost in a sea of froth. They lose the benefits of long-term appreciation.

The real problem with institutional managers, though, is pure ego. In their frenzy to beat the person in the next office they forget for whom they really work. Portfolio managers in big mutual fund companies may easily forget the client, especially since they don't even know the client. They end up in such a mutually destructive competition with their fellow managers that they lose sight of the fact that it isn't their money.

All this is facilitated by communications technology, which tends to overwhelm fund managers with far more information than they truly know what to do with. Because they can't separate what is important from what is not, they become skittish, superstitious, and fearful that another fund manager might be up 2.9 percent for the week instead of 2.8 percent. That one-tenth-of-1-percent difference is so galling, they start trading frantically to catch up—hence the market's furious churning for no apparent reason.

This is foolish. The only people who consistently come out ahead in such markets are people who ignore noise in favor of taking a long-term view. If a fund manager is running a lower-than-average-risk portfolio and is one-tenth of a percentage point behind the person next door, so what? This strategy shouldn't be expected to do as well at the very end of a bull market as a growth-stock portfolio. In fact, it shouldn't be doing as well, because that means it's taking too much risk. Eventually a bear market will come, and when it does, the defensive portfolio will decline far less than that of the others down the hall.

If you pay attention to the meaningless noise generated by frantic institutional managers you'll go crazy, because you're trying to understand something that you assume is rational when in fact it's caused by nothing more than the ego, jealousy, and fear of a deeply insecure portfolio manager desperately trying to overcome the one-tenth-of-1-percent advantage enjoyed by the associates next door.

The Case Against Data Mining

Some people have spent their whole lives trying to figure out what causes the market to go up and down. The simplistic model is that bad news makes the model go down and good news makes it go up. However, what is good news and what is bad news is very subjective.

Before Reagan, one could prove mathematically that Democrats were good for the stock market and Republicans were terrible. If you sat there and said, "Okay, Ronald Reagan has been elected, therefore we are going to have one of the great bear markets of all time" and then proceeded to invest on that basis, you would have had your head handed to you.

Today, when you do the numbers, you see it doesn't make any difference. Before Reagan, we had Hoover and Roosevelt. Hoover was clearly bad and Roosevelt was terrific for stocks.

Would Hoover have been terrible if he had started at 80 like Roosevelt did instead of at 300? Would Roosevelt have been terrific if he had started at 300 instead of 80? The level you start from makes a big difference in rate of return.

If you are going to do an analysis on the economy, you have to distinguish between after-the-fact rationalization and causality. Both are different from correlations. With computers, anyone can mine the data to find two things that are closely correlated. The problem is the correlation most likely is totally meaningless. There is no causality; one doesn't proceed from the other. Most of what passes today for news may indeed be factual, but there is no causality there either. As a result you end up with all sorts of spurious conclusions.

Most of today's facts have been built on ten years of data, because most databases give ten years of data. Is it better to use a database based on ten years than another number of years when trying to predict something? Experience says no. But that is what most people want you to do. They say, "Well, it was true for the last ten years. Why won't it be true for the next ten?" You'd be better off just flipping a coin.

I'm not saying it's not good to be optimistic. The most successful investors always are. However, there comes a point when you have to unplug the bubble machine. Analysis of trends can only take you so far. Eventually you simply have to say, "I don't care what the trend is. I don't want any technical analysis. All I need to know is whether or not it's cheap. If it's cheap, I'll buy it."

You Don't Have to Go for Broke

Now that you've decided to buy, you next have to decide how much. There's no rule that says you have to buy all at once.

Maybe you have money for 300 shares. So to start, you buy 100 shares. If it goes cheaper, you buy another 100 shares. If it goes even cheaper, you buy the remaining 100 shares. Now if it goes cheaper than that, maybe the stock is trying to tell you something, so you don't buy anything (and you're out of money, in any case). But if it comes up just a little bit, then you start looking for money to buy some more.

What if the stock is headed for the toilet? At this point, it is not a financial decision. Most people are worried about risk, and I for one wouldn't try to talk them out of it. But if you are looking for maximum return, I can argue pretty persuasively that when a stock goes down you buy. If it goes down again you buy more. If it keeps going down you keep on buying. Such a strategy leaves most people so terrified they just won't do it, which is too bad.

It's very common to see a stock go from 30 to 25 to 20. If you invest all your money at 20, what happens when it goes to 15? Well, most likely you feel like an idiot—at great effort and expense you've fought your way on board a sinking ship. But if you hold on long enough, eventually the stock will get back to 30, at which point you aren't an idiot anymore. The problem is that most people wouldn't have waited that long. The instant the stock went from 15 to 20, they would have been so relieved to get back their losses, they would have unloaded the whole lot.

Spare's Conservation of Risk Principle

Sometimes as investment advisors we have to do things that keep us from being Number One. The good news is that they also keep us from being Number Five. If we are consistently Number Two or Number Three, that's fine. This doesn't have anything to do with right and wrong. It's more just a certain consistency of attitude, a basic principle: if we take a risk, we take it in stock.

The rest of the assets we generally put in treasury securities. If the spread between treasuries and corporates gets wide enough, we will on occasion buy corporates. We don't like to do it. All things being equal, we'd prefer to take our risk in stocks.

There is nothing right or wrong about this. It's not something carved in stone. This is just the way we view risk, but we think it's important. If a client says, "No. We should be in there for every quarter of a percent difference," that person won't be our client for very long.

As investment advisors, we have to be honest with ourselves and our customers. We don't want to surprise our customers and we don't want to be surprised by them. If we have had a client for ten years and something goes haywire in the market and suddenly the client pulls out all his or her money in two months, then we have to tune up our antenna, because we weren't listening to our client carefully enough.

We don't blame the client when something like this happens. It's the client's money. He or she has to do what's right for him or her, subject to hearing our advice. If the client says, "Well, all that is nice, but I don't agree with it," and goes off on his or her merry way, that's fine. It's the client's right. When it comes to investing, a financial advisor should never pressure a client to do anything with which the client isn't comfortable.

—◢◣◢◣—

CHAPTER 7

Formulating Your Personal Investment Philosophy

$\mathbf{M}$any people in the investment business refer to themselves as "professional investors." It's a phrase that always makes me wince. The investment business is not a profession. Being a doctor is a profession; being a lawyer is a profession.

Investing is no more a science than sociology is a science, which is to say there's a lot of information out there, with a lot of theories about what it all means and very few that actually work.

The biggest problem "professional" investors have is too much information, most of which is garbage. We are expected to know what is happening minute to minute, have all the facts, and be on top of every development at every company. The people who expect this of us are the people who for the most part don't have a clue.

This is where the individual investor has a big advantage. You don't have fifty people calling you one hundred times a day and asking about what is happening today, yesterday, or tomorrow ("What's the forecast?"). You have an opportunity to focus on a longer time frame and to cut out all this intermediary noise. You have the chance to achieve a little clarity.

How do you achieve clarity?

Start by looking back at the previous twenty years. Basically, you want to look at the middle and find the average. What's the normal history? Is the history likely to recur?

I'm writing this at the beginning of 1997. We have had a bull market since August of 1982. The Dow started at 720; by early 1997, it was at 6700. Most likely, the next fourteen years will be the opposite. It's happened before. Between March of 1965 (when I started in the investment business) and August of 1982, nothing happened for seventeen years. Stocks were 870 on the Dow, plus or minus 100 points, 80 percent of the time. For seventeen years, it was nothing—zero, zilch. You sat there and collected the dividend. Conditions like that do not continue forever.

Will the market get to 7000 by the end of the 1997? Who knows?

Are we overvalued? Yes. On a six-month basis? Who knows? Five years? Yes. Twenty years? Probably not.

The other thing you should do is try not to be too precise. In my 1992 book, *Relative Dividend Yield*, I point out that our firm has always taken the point of view that we would rather be roughly right than precisely wrong. Most people try to buy low and sell high, which is very hard to do. People try to do that all the time, and few people succeed. Switch it around, and it's much more doable. Instead of trying to buy low, just make sure you don't sell near the bottom. Instead of trying to sell high, just make sure you don't buy near the top.

Here's an example: Suppose the market is currently overvalued on a five-year horizon, and you have an unexpected windfall that you want to invest. What do you do?

Well, there isn't any law that says you have to do 100 percent of anything. If you don't know what to do, only do a little. If you have 80 percent of your portfolio in stocks and you are uncomfortable because you think the market is currently overvalued, then you don't have to eliminate your stocks altogether—have 75 percent.

If you are afraid of the market and you don't own any stocks, go out and buy 5 percent. You don't have to own zero.

Spare's Principle of Temporal Tumult

Don't listen to short-term noise. Pay attention to the long term, but then act in a reasonable manner.

When in Doubt, Invest Mechanically

In December of 1995, one of my high school classmates called me. His aunt had died and left him $300,000 in cash. He asked me what to do.

At the time, the market seemed to me to be overvalued. Assuming he wanted to be fully vested in two years, would there be at least the start of a bear market in the next two years? I decided yes, probably. Two years would be long enough, then. So that would be $1/24$ every month under normal conditions. However, since the market was overvalued, I told him to buy only $1/48$ every month. Then, when the market looked normal, he should buy $1/24$. Once he got into the bear market and stock started to get cheap, he should raise the buying rate to $1/12$ a month.

Recently I saw him again. The first thing he said was, "What should we do in this crazy market?" It was obvious he still had all his money 100 percent in cash, which is too bad. He was afraid to jump into the market when it was high for fear he'd buy at the top, get hit with a correction, and see the value of his investment suddenly cut in half. On the other hand, if he waited until the market hit bottom he wouldn't invest then either, because he would be too afraid it would fall even more.

If you're scared to invest at the top because you're afraid of a correction and scared to invest at the bottom for fear of a depression, you never do invest and you miss out on the fact that common stocks have achieved a total average return of 10 percent a year over the last seventy years.

I'm not advising you to rush into anything. If you really think you have thirty, thirty-five, or forty years to live, why be in a hurry to put together your portfolio today? Two years is no big deal, time-wise. But if you keep putting off getting into the market until the perfect moment arrives, it never will— even if it did, you'd probably chicken out anyway. You are much better off being relatively mechanical about getting invested.

I'm not saying you should go out and do straight dollar cost averaging (spending a set amount on stock every month, irrespective of the stock's price). I don't believe that you should buy $\frac{1}{24}$ a month for two years regardless of value. If the market is expensive, do $\frac{1}{48}$ instead. If it is cheap, you may want to do $\frac{1}{12}$. If it is fair-valued, you might want to do $\frac{1}{24}$. You don't have to do it all at one time, but you want to be doing something all the time.

The Case for God Time

The great *Life* magazine photographer Alfred Eisenstaedt was once asked to explain the difference between a snapshot and a great photograph. His answer: "About three inches."

That positioning—two inches over, one inch higher—can make all the difference in the world. This point of view has always had a lot of appeal to me, because it seems so small ("Three inches? Who cares?"), yet when you look at the result, it's the difference between a banal snapshot and real art.

My friend, the late photographer Wynn Bullock, liked to talk about shadow, foreground, light, and dark, which are very important in photography. A two-dimensional photograph has a three-dimensional quality to it only if you get shadows, foreground, background, and lighting. Once, I was down at his house in Monterey, and the discussion got around to whether or not the earth was created in six days. His fourteen-year-old daughter said something very insightful: "It was six days, but it was God time." That really struck me. It's a matter of perspective.

To get perspective on the stock market, moving three inches to one side doesn't help. But instead of looking one month, one quarter, or one year ahead, look three to five years ahead, and you'll see things from a totally different perspective.

In my experience, most people go from one extreme to the other. Either they focus on the very short term or they look ahead twenty years. They tend not to land very often in the three- to five-year time period. Now it's not precisely three to five; sometimes it's three to seven. Something in the middle works better in the long run than the extremes. Most investors and all TV talking heads think in 100 percent or zero terms. In reality, you never get the end of life as we know it and you never get limitless prosperity. The truth tends to lie in the middle. It's simply not true that people in the middle get run over from both sides.

Watching Out for Investor Attitudes

When evaluating the market, we have found that three to five years works for us at the firm. Not only is it the market cycle, it's a business-decision cycle. By the time a company gets cheap, the problem is generally well known. At this point, the company has to find the problem, design a fix, and carry it out.

A small company can figure out what's wrong in six months. It may take another six months to design the fix and another year to carry it out. Big companies may take a year or more to even pinpoint why things have gone bad. Then they take another year deciding what to do about it and a couple more years to solve the problem. This is why investors need to look ahead three to five years, especially when buying large company stocks.

With a small company, we like to buy our stock within the first three months, or certainly no later than the first six months, after the stock gets cheap. If you wait for more information, you're going to lose the opportunity. Cheap stocks are from companies with problems. As soon as the stock gets cheap, we start to buy. Because we (generally) only buy stocks with high relative dividend yields, we are being paid to wait. Typically it doesn't take long for the management to turn these medium-sized companies around, so when they go cheap you have to move fast. Some companies will recover share price in a single year. Most companies take longer, but you can't sit around—if you don't get in when the stock is cheap you won't make any money. Investor attitudes swing on a dime.

The Fallacy of Precision

In investing, there is such a thing as knowing too much. Having too many facts does not give you knowledge. Knowing theory without knowing what is good or bad from the theory isn't useful. It might give you nice lecture notes, but it doesn't

let you run the country or invest money successfully or anything else. Brains alone are not the criteria.

This is not a call for stupid investment managers or
stupid politicians or stupid anything. I'm merely pointing out
that just being smart is not enough. A lot of other factors are
involved, and most of them are psychological and behavioral.

There's a power curve in investment knowledge. You
want to know enough about a given stock that it makes a difference. So you double your effort, and that gets you from 50
percent to 97 percent. But the second doubling of effort only
gets you from 97 percent to 99 percent. That's not a good
deal, particularly if you are dealing with an inherent lack of
precision to begin with. If you can't measure success within
five or ten percentage points, why bother breaking your neck
to try and get it down to two? You can't tell whether you've
done anything or not. So you work on stuff you know you are
going to succeed at and don't bother with the rest.

If It's Not Right for You, It Isn't Right

Although I personally believe in common stocks (especially
cheap ones) and our investment management firm devotes
much of its interest to common stocks, I'm not by any means
saying that everyone should have all their assets in common
stocks or even necessarily any of them. A portfolio has to
match your personality as well as your current and future
financial conditions. Some people might be better in bonds,
T-bills, or real estate.

My father was an attorney and developer in Chicago. He
built the first motel on Lake Shore Drive. Although his
specialty was real estate, he also invested in stocks. I'm not
sure why though, because to him they were just pieces of

paper that were quoted in the newspaper every day. Riding the train home from work every day, he read the *Sun Times, Daily News,* and *Chicago Tribune* and computed his net worth in his head. The sudden changes drove him crazy. To him, real estate made far more sense.

I once was in his office when the subject of the price of land between Phoenix and Tucson came up. My father called an Arizona broker to ask what the land was worth. It was about $1,500 per acre. He then asked what it could sell for. The answer was $950 an acre.

I sat there and said, "Whoa." But it didn't make any difference to my father—the fact that the selling price and the value were two vastly different numbers didn't bother him at all. That's when it first dawned on me: being a successful real estate investor involved totally different thought processes than being a successful stock investor.

My father went on to make a lot of money in real estate, but the only people who made money on his stock portfolio were his brokers. They really took advantage of him. They turned over and transacted him to death. Finally, when I was about twenty-four years old, he let me take care of the stocks. He recognized that stock investing was simply not his forte. And that's why I say there are some people who should never own stocks, some who should never own bonds, some who should never have cash, and some who should never have real estate.

My personal opinion is that common stocks (especially cheap stocks) offer the best long-term prospects for maximizing one's wealth. But there are times when you might also want cash, T-bill bonds, or real estate. You can't put a portfolio together by some formula. You have to match your portfolio with your personality, your age, your circumstances, and your life. It's you who defines what is right or wrong, not the broker and not some elitist group. If it's not right for you, it isn't right.

Switching Philosophies Midstream

At the beginning of 1997, the S&P 500 stood at 775. Is the market overvalued? Yes. When the market drops, the same thing will happen that always happens during a correction: panic will set in. And there's nothing we can we do about it. Each investor has to go through the experience individually and react in his or her own way.

All that I can do at our investment firm is to try and establish a mind-set that this is a chance to learn rather than to give up and fall apart. I regularly point out that sudden drops in the market are inevitable so that when they do occur people won't throw up their hands in panic. Basically, the way you cope with crises is to plan for market corrections ahead of time so when they occur you will have a more even keel than the world around you. And I don't just mean corrections where the market falls. People can lose their heads when the market is going up sharply too. Whether the market is up or down, I want to be at the smoother center point.

To some degree, really long-term investors are in the middle of a teeter totter; when the market moves, they are going to have to move some too. But you don't want to be playing Crack-the-Whip—you just don't want those extreme movements at either end. The people who do that will just end up emotional basket cases, and the best way to avoid that is to decide ahead of time where you want to sit. Do you want to sit at the end, where the ride might be a little wild? Or do you want to sit more toward the middle, where you have more time to think?

Trend followers and extrapolators are the people who end up out at the ends. When the market is going up, to them that is the best time to own stock. When the market is going down, that's the best time not to. They know when they've hit bottom because the bottom is where they were before they started going up. They know when they've reached the top because that's where the market was before it went down.

There is nothing wrong with people who think this way— if they are speculators and traders. In fact, I would go even further to say that speculators and traders have to think this way. Speculators think differently than investors. To them, trading activity over short time horizons isn't risky. That is their world. They live in it. They understand it, and for them it's no problem.

What I object to is people who think like that and call themselves investors, because they aren't. If you are a trader/trend follower/speculator, then proudly say, "I am a speculator." On the other hand, if you have a five- or ten- or twenty-year investment time horizon, then you can say, "I am an investor." What you don't want to do is take an investor and suddenly put him or her in a speculator's chair, because that's just asking for trouble. By the same token, a speculator in an investor's chair is also out of place.

If you are a short-term (three to six months) thinker and it works for you, then fine, keep doing it. Even if you're not making a killing, at least you aren't always having to fight your instincts. The problem with most people is that they switch at the wrong time. When the market gets near the top, they suddenly become long-term investors; when the market gets near the bottom, they suddenly become short-term speculators.

In theory there's nothing wrong with switching from one market strategy to another—if thereafter you stick to the new approach. But most people don't have the discipline to stay with the program long enough for it to work. They hold on to cheap stocks for two or three years, and when nothing happens, they convince themselves it was all a mistake, whereupon they suddenly become trend-following, momentum buyers. Then when they go to parties they can talk about owning all the same high-priced glamour stocks that all their friends do, except they almost invariably switch too late—they buy at a peak and get creamed when the stock declines.

At this point, they should decide never to change again, which would be fine because they would still have twenty or thirty years to recover. But in reality most people don't stay with any one strategy over the long run. They want so much to be in fashion and in tune with everyone else that they move to cheap-stock buying ("value investing" in today's institutional vernacular) when it's in fashion and abandon it when it's not. Those people are just doomed to be financial losers because they can't stick with a consistent discipline and invariably switch at the wrong time.

It takes a certain amount of character to buy stocks that everyone is rushing to unload, to hold on to them for two or four years during which they may do absolutely nothing, and then to sell them once they start to rise, just as everyone else is jumping on board clamoring to buy. To most people this is just too counterintuitive.

It's true. It takes patience. It takes discipline. And it takes a willingness to accept a slightly lower rate of return in very-fast-rising bull markets, because you know you'll more than make up the difference when the inevitable bear market or "normal" market comes along.

Buying on Despair, Selling on Excitement

Too often I think investors fall into despair for no good reason. If the market is cheap, don't be pessimistic. Don't assume it's the end of the world. Don't listen to rumors that we will never exist as an industrial society again. I'm not advising you to bury your head in the sand. It's good to be reasonably pessimistic. But if a stock still looks cheap, and you know it's a good value for your retirement portfolio, go ahead and buy it. This is true whether you know what the absolute bottom is or not.

Look at the period from 1929 to 1932. The market was clearly overvalued at 200, 300, 390. And it was cheap at 100, 80, 60, 40. You could say since the market is undervalued at 80 to 100, it would be a mistake to sell—and you would be right. If your goal is merely not to sell when the market is cheap, not selling at 80 is perfectly fine. The fact that the market subsequently went down to 42 doesn't matter. It was only there for a little while and 80 was still cheap.

Human psychology has a lot to do with how people react to market changes. Many people regard losses as unfair and gains as their God-given right. When earnings are terrific, people at first are pleasantly surprised, but they quickly get over it and pretty soon these new highs become the standard from which they extrapolate the future.

Most people, I've found, don't think clearly about risk. Although there is far more risk in a market that is overvalued than in one that has just undergone a correction, most people act as if the opposite were true. People were far more concerned in July 1996 when the market fell to 5300 than they were a few weeks earlier when the market was at 5700. They get the most concerned when the market hits bottom. In fact, that's why you get bottoms—people freak out when the market starts to decline and dump all their stocks. I don't pretend to know what the bottom is for the current market, but whatever it is, I can guarantee you that when it comes most people will see far less opportunity in it than they will at a market peak. And that, if you think about it, is a real tough way to make money.

At the beginning of 1997, the Dow was at 6700. Since the market was overvalued, were all stocks therefore expensive? Some were, and some weren't. It wasn't a universal. But could you have found a diversified list of cheap stocks? Absolutely. Remember: if you are going to focus on cheap stocks, don't fool around. If you believe in the strategy, then stay with it. If the index has dropped 20 percent and your portfolio is only down 5 percent, terrific.

Most investors love stocks when they are at their price peaks and hate them at their bottoms. How are you going to make money if you love a stock at 55, hate it at 30, and love it all the more at 60? That's a tough way to make a living. People justify this kind of a strategy by rationalizing their passions. "Well, I didn't like it at 30," they will say, "but boy have they gotten their act together." So they buy it at 40 and play it till 60. That's one way to do it. It's the hard way, but it is one way.

Our firm takes a different approach. Because we buy on despair and sell on excitement, we're not alarmed when a stock that used to be at 55 goes down to 32. We see it as an opportunity: "It's at 32? That's cheap! Let's buy a few shares." Then we buy a few more at 30, and buy even more at 29. We average it out. We're cheap-stock buyers.

Giving Away Secrets

One thing that always makes me suspicious is when a competitor stands up and tells us how he does what he does. Why would a competitor reveal his professional secrets if they were really any good? Yet here we are doing the same thing—laying out all our professional secrets for all the world to see.

The reason it doesn't bother us is that we are not just laying out a set of rules in this book. We are offering an entire philosophy of investing. That's why we can show the competition everything we do and it still won't help them. That would require them to change their entire investment philosophy, and frankly most of them are simply not about to do that.

It's not that we are brilliant and they're not. It's not that we have the inside track and they don't. It's really our attitude. Our methods depend on having longer time horizons than most people in this business think are reasonable or required. One of the people who trained me once suggested that someone who holds a stock for anything less than five years may be considered an intelligent speculator but is still far short of being an investor. And, you know, he is right.

Investors who spend their time worrying about what is going to happen next week or next month make some really poor decisions. Many portfolio managers sell stock at the wrong time just so they can have more pleasant quarterly performance meetings with their clients. Holding a nonperforming stock is so embarrassing to some portfolio managers that they can only deal with it by selling the stock. They don't want to tell a client that their portfolio is down.

We don't like bad news either. Some of the cheap stocks we buy just sit there for years (although in compensation our clients are collecting some very high dividend yields). In the end, cheap stocks deliver. That's when our clients make money, and that's when we do too.

Flashy Stocks and Daring Traders

We know cheap stocks are boring to a lot of people. We know they're unpopular. We know it is not really socially acceptable to do what we do—you can't be a cheap-stock investor and go to cocktail parties and dazzle everyone with stories about the zoomy computer or software stock you just bought. If you tell them what you really own, you'll end up in the corner talking to yourself.

Even so, I'm often surprised that more people aren't nervous about buying fashionable stocks at the tail ends of bull markets. They know the market isn't cheap. I know they don't believe in it, but for some reason they think they have to play.

Oftentimes they end up paying for the privilege. Because the specialists are always running out of money at tops and bottoms, bull markets are more dangerous now than they used to be. When things are working well, specialists are supposed to take the other side of a trade to smooth things out. This is to ensure that a stock sale that might have caused a stock to go down half a point now only results in a quarter-point drop. The problem today is that brokerage firms are still committing the same amount of capital to their specialist accounts that they used to commit fifteen years ago, even though today's market is three to five times as high. This makes the market potentially far more volatile once it changes direction.

Avoiding Zoomy Stocks in the Tail End of Bull Markets

Institutional clients sometimes hire us as defensive value managers, then turn around and wonder why we don't do really well in the tail ends of bull markets—until we get a big two- or three-week drop as we did in July of 1996. Then they suddenly remember why they originally hired us. The cavalry does arrive just in time. Sometimes the bugle is muted, but help was there all the time over the hill and eventually arrives.

There's a good reason why value (cheap-stock) managers don't generally do well in bull markets: investor attitudes are so ebullient, it's hard to find as many underloved cheap stocks to buy. During the first six months of 1996, the market was up every month. It's not normal to have that kind of run—even in a bull market.

Then at the tail ends of bull markets you get price spikes. Instead of a broad advance where all the stocks go up a little, you start to see a very narrow advance where just a few stocks go up a lot. Because cheap-stock investors tend not to own stocks that zoom up and down like this, other investors will sometimes look at those peaks and conclude we aren't doing very well. We are in fact doing well—just not in the short term. Stocks that go up real fast will come down real fast.

Where Should the Market Be?

It's hard to know where the market should be, because it seldom ends up in the middle. It is usually overvalued or undervalued, and it typically only hits the middle going from one extreme to the other.

The mania of 1995 and 1996 has also made the market more extreme. In 1995, the indexes were up almost 40 percent. The Dow was up 37 percent. There have only been three times in the history of the Dow where it went up 40 percent or more: 1933, 1935, and 1954. For 1996, the indexes were up another 23 percent. That's a lot.

Where should the market be if it were appropriately valued? If you are taking the long view, look at the average postwar yield: 3½ percent. The dividend is currently something like $14.80 on the S&P 500, which is below trend. Normally you'd expect it to be around $18.50. If you take that number and divide it by .035, you find that the S&P 500 should really be at about 530 today.

It is actually at 775 or thereabouts. You bet it is overvalued. Most people are pretty good at figuring out whether the market is overvalued, undervalued, or fairly valued on a one- or two-year basis. The problem occurs when they start extrapolating downward to oblivion or upward toward infinity. Instead of trying to figure out whether stocks will get cheaper or whether the market has hit bottom, they should concentrate on something much easier: is the market cheap? If it's cheap, don't sell. Even if the market goes down further, don't sell.

You can decide when the market is overvalued in very gross terms. It's a simple matter of doing a little normalization (comparing it to long-term trends). Buying at bottom (or selling at top) is a lot harder—it implies there's a way to figure that out.

One way to protect yourself is to be as optimistic as you reasonably can when the market is overvalued. Then at the bottom you want to be just as reasonably pessimistic. You want to stretch it out so you really are not caught buying stock way above the bottom. Just be sure you don't use price-to-earnings ratios. From 1990 to 1992, the Dow dividends dropped from 115 to 90 and the earnings dropped from 140 or 150 to 60. If you did a price-earnings when earnings were at 60, you discovered the Dow was selling at twenty-seven times earnings.

That's pure nonsense. The Dow wasn't at twenty-seven times normal earnings back in 1990–92. It was at twenty-seven times *depressed* earnings. It was a pretty easy thing to guess that PEs had to decline because earnings were bound to go up. Prices also rose. PEs didn't tell you everything. The market wasn't overvalued at twenty-seven times, nor is it cheap today with a PE of 18. Earnings went from way below trend—$60—to way above trend—$320 on the Dow.

The dividends are slowly catching up with the Dow, going from $90 to about $125. Normal is probably about $150. Where should the market be? If you divide normal dividends by the post–World War II rate average yield, you end up with a Dow of about 4300. At the beginning of 1997, the Dow was actually 6700, which was overvalued. That was not taking today's dividends as reported either. That was allowing for maximum optimism.

On the downside, the market was cheap in 1990–92, even if you said the dividends would be $80 instead of $90.

If it looks like the market is overvalued, you want to push the numbers as high as you can. If you find the market is overvalued on optimistic numbers, then it is really overvalued.

Falling for Fluorescent Laces

If you ask the average investment advisor what the two main categories of stocks are, he or she will tell you growth stocks and value stocks.

That is one distinction. Unfortunately, it's just not a very useful one. For one thing, there is no such thing as a valueless investor. No professional investor ever says, "I only buy expensive stocks and I don't care what they cost." The client would be justifiably wary ("What do you mean you don't care about value?").

Still, in practice, most investors ignore value and follow market trends, which is to say they buy the same stocks everyone else is buying (and thus guarantee them to be overpriced). Today we call them momentum players. In less euphemistic times we simply called them believers in the "greater fool" theory: they didn't mind paying more for a stock than it was worth because they figured no matter what they paid they could always find a greater fool to sell it to for even more money.

This is not to say we never buy growth stocks. Although our firm concentrates on cheap stocks, we also buy small growth stocks when they are cheap. Our time horizon on our growth stocks is ten years plus, which is to say we don't buy anything if we don't think there is a ten year potential. Sometimes the price of these stocks goes up enough that we have to sell them in two or three years, but we don't go into any situation looking for the quick hit. We are not interested in fads and we are not interested in style. We are not interested in LA Gear just because they have fluorescent laces.

The trick is to distinguish a growth stock from a faddish stock. Is Nike a style/fad business or is it not? When Nike started out, it looked pretty faddish. Now it can probably be considered a company of size and substance. Coca-Cola, fifty or sixty years ago, was probably considered a fad. Since you can't always tell fads from substance, sometimes you just have to wait. Sometimes you get opportunities to buy Coca-Cola cheap. Cheap tends to be unpopular. Cheap and unpopular kind of go together. The distinction isn't value stocks versus growth stocks. It's popular versus unpopular; it's faddish versus substantial; it's love versus neglect.

CHAPTER 8

———◊◊◊———

Dealing with
a Professional

If, after reading the foregoing chapters, you have concluded that the do-it-yourself approach just isn't for you and that your investments would be better off in the hands of a professional, you will still need to do your own research and homework. Investment advisors are simply advisors. They will guide you and give you information, but the final decision should always be up to you.

Although people outside the business sometimes assume that professional investors are very bright, passionate people who know exactly what they're doing, I have found that most people have entered the field because (1) it was socially acceptable, and (2) it paid well. In truth 85 percent of them don't know what they're doing. When you ask them why they picked a particular stock, they can't tell you. Or, more importantly, if you ask them how the various stocks in their portfolio are related, their answer, when stripped to its essentials, is that "a portfolio is simply a bunch of stocks." They can't

---

An Aside to Investment Managers

You probably think you've been hired because you are pretty smart, you went to good schools, you have a gift of gab, and your performance has been good. Wrong. You're a target. You are somebody the company has hired in order to have someone to fire if something ever goes wrong.

In a bull market, of course, there aren't any problems.

---

explain what factor drives the choice, because they have no criteria. They can't explain why they own what they own.

I'm not saying a portfolio ought to consist only of high yield stocks or only of growth stocks, but it should at least have some semblance of orderliness. In our private client accounts, we own stocks from zero yield to utilities yielding 10 percent. They are all, however, cheap stocks. That is the driver. Most investment managers unfortunately don't have a consistent theory of investing. They don't know why their portfolios act the way they do when the market changes. Consequently they get blown all over the place every time the wind shifts. I mean, how do you know if you are reaching your goals if you don't know where you are starting from or where you want to end up?

How to Pick an Investment Advisor

The most important factor to consider when selecting an investment advisor is comfort. You have to trust that the person you hire understands your needs, goals, risk tolerance, and financial intelligence. To get good investment advice, you have to be willing to reveal and express your ideas to someone who both understands you and will keep your thoughts confidential.

Be sure the person you pick knows something about both up and down markets. At SKB&A, we have investment managers in their twenties, thirties, forties, and fifties. Young people have great energy and inquisitiveness but may lack perspective because we've been in a bull market for the last fourteen years. On the other hand, some of us in our fifties may be too concerned about the bear markets of the past. A balance is both important and stimulating.

Beware of any investment advisor who has his or her interests at heart rather than your own. If an advisor is churning your account to generate commissions, watch out. If he says that an investment is a slam dunk that he bought for his own grandmothers, forget it.

Some advisors view their customers as just hamburger to be used for the benefit of shareholders or senior management. That's never appropriate. One doesn't *use* customers. One becomes *useful* to customers. The client really must come first. It is not a bad thing to be a financial servant, which is really what we are if we are doing the job properly. We are in there with the lawyers and the accountants and the tax attorneys—we're all financial servants.

At SKB&A, once we know the client's expectations, risk tolerances, and general attitudes toward money, then we go about the job of building accounts. It is a process of give and take, and it is always going back and forth. One size never fits all. Any advisors you hire should be able to explain what they do and why they do it. If you ask a reasonable question, you should get a reasonable answer. If they can't give you an answer, find someone who can.

Our firm doesn't work for nothing, but at least our attitude is that if we take care of the clients, they will take care of us, and not the other way around. If you find a financial advisor or broker who doesn't listen to your point of view and address your needs, then get rid of that person, because there is no single right portfolio or single right anything. If it isn't right for you, it isn't right.

Types of Financial Advisor

There are two types of professionals who can help you with your retirement needs: financial planners, who will help you draw up a retirement plan (or check one you've drawn up yourself), and investment advisors, who will help you manage your assets to best achieve your retirement goals.

Financial Planners

Financial planners are the generalists of this field. They help individuals delineate their financial strategies, taking into consideration each client's specific objectives. They also aid clients in coordinating their various financial concerns.

If you decide a financial planner is what you need, here are some factors you may want to consider in hiring one:

- Check on the financial planner's formal educational background, professional training, and continuing scholarship.

- Make sure you understand what methods of compensation the planner will expect for his or her work.

- Seek a planner who has clients with situations similar to your own.

● Ask for references.

● Read the financial planner's brochure and/or the ADV form required for registration with the Securities and Exchange Commission. This should disclose extensive information on the financial planner and his or her practice, including philosophy, practice structure, fees, and potential conflicts of interest.

Following is a guide to the qualifications of various types of financial planners.

CFP (Chartered Financial Planner): The International Board of Standards and Practices for Certified Financial Planners (based in Denver, Colorado) awards this title to planners who complete an accepted course, pass a special test, and meet certain additional requirements, including work-related experience.

CPA/PFS (Certified Public Accountant/Personal Financial Specialist): The American Institute of Certified Public Accountants (based in New York) awards this title to CPAs who have passed a special exam and meet certain additional requirements.

ChFC (Chartered Financial Consultant): This title is designated by the American College (Bryn Mawr, Pennsylvania) to consultants who complete a special ten-part course of study. They must also meet certain other professional requirements.

If you need more information about planners, the following professional organizations can provide select listings of financial planners in your area and related information:

The American Institute of CPAs can provide a list of CPA/PFS financial planners. Telephone (800) 862-4272.

The Institute of Certified Financial Planners will provide a roll of financial planners with CFP designation. Telephone (800) 282-7526.

The International Association for Financial Planning (IAFP) will send a list, called "The Registry," of financial planners who have fulfilled certain IAFP qualification requirements. Telephone (404) 395-1605.

The International Board of Standards and Practices for Certified Financial Planners will certify that a financial planner has earned CFP designation and remains in good standing. Telephone (303) 830-7543.

LINC (Licensed Independent Network of CPA Financial Planners) will furnish a list of fee-only financial planners in public accounting firms. Telephone (615) 782-4240.

The National Association of Personal Financial Advisors will supply a list of fee-only financial planners. Telephone (800) 366-2732.

Investment Advisors

Investment advisors (also called investment consultants, counselors, or money managers) manage assets, making portfolio and individual investment decisions at their own inclination. They can range from independent advisory firms to bank trust departments.

Getting performance information on advisors may be more difficult than getting information on planners. Private money managers work with numerous, different accounts for which different individuals may be responsible; there is no publicly available information on those accounts, making performance measurement difficult.

In looking for an investment advisor, make sure that the performance numbers you inspect are generated by the individual(s) planning to manage your investments. Make sure your portfolio will be individually tailored and not part of an investment blend.

Following are the professional designations for investment advisors, consultants, and counselors.

AIMC (Chartered Investment Management Consultant): This is designated by the Institute for Investment Management Consultants (Phoenix, Arizona) to Institute members upon completion of an investment administration consulting course.

CFA (Chartered Financial Analyst): This title is denoted by the Association of Investment Management Research (based in Charlottesville, Virginia) to those who satisfy a rigorous three-level examination. Each level of the exam is taken in consecutive years. The exam, administered by the Association, covers investment principles, analysis, and administration. CFAs must also meet certain additional requirements, including a bachelor's degree or equivalent professional work background and three years of investment decision experience.

CIC (Chartered Investment Counselor): Designated by the Investment Counsel Association of America (based in New York) to those holding CFAs who function as investment counselors and fulfill certain additional professional requirements.

CIMA (Certified Investment Management Analyst): This is designated by the Investment Management Consultants Association (based in Denver, Colorado) to consultants who complete a one-week course at Wharton, pass the special exam, and satisfy certain additional professional requirements.

CIMC (Certified Investment Management Consultant): The Institute for Investment Management Consultants designates this title to members with more professional counseling experience than the AIMC. They meet certain additional requirements as well.

The following professional associations will provide select lists of investment consultants in your area.

The Institute for Investment Management Consultants will provide a list of investment AIMC or CIMC consultants. Telephone (602) 265-6114.

The Investment Management Consultants Association will provide a list of investment consultants with the CIMA designation. Telephone (303) 770-3377.

The following publications cover registered investment analysts. Several are geared toward the institutional industry (pension fund and endowments) and include managers with account minimums over $1 million. They are all available for purchase, but some may also be found in public and business school libraries.

CDA/Cadence, 1355 Piccard Drive, Suite 220, Rockville, MD 20850; telephone (800) 833-1394. CDA's Investment Advisor Performance Survey provides analyst performance measurements based on information provided by the investment analysts. It includes phone numbers and information on how to reach analysts as well.

Directory of Registered Investment Advisors with the SEC, Money Market Directories, 320 East Main Street, Charlottesville, VA 22902; telephone (804) 977-1450 (or 800-446-2810 if you live in Virginia). Directory includes nearly 6,000 SEC-registered analysts listed according to state. The criteria is SEC registration, so some of the firms included do not necessarily oversee money (they may include newsletters, planners, and stockbrokers). Performance data is not included.

Money Manager Review, 1550 California Street, Suite 263, San Francisco, CA 94109; telephone (415) 386-7111. This publication tracks about 800 investment analysts based on performance information furnished by the analysts themselves. It publishes information on the prime 15 percent of analysts, ranked by performance over five years. All are compared with others in their own risk groups. One section provides short, personalized reports on the managers covered.

Nelson's Directory of Investment Managers, Nelson Publications, One Gateway Plaza, P.O. Box 591, Port Chester, NY 10573; telephone (914) 937-8400. This provides a listing of about 2,000 analysts who actively administer assets on a fully independent basis. It focuses primarily on those with large minimums who control institutional (pension plan) assets. Listings usually include annual return figures based on manager-supplied information.

The Interview

Most individuals interview prospective advisors before making a selection. Typically, advisors offer a free initial one-hour consultation to potential clients. This generosity isn't purely altruistic—they also want to screen you to determine whether their firm should accept you as a client. You should exploit this free interview to see if you are comfortable with the advisor. Note whether the advisor asks questions about your goals and objectives. If the questioning centers mostly on one particular financial area (for instance, your insurance programs), you may be talking to someone who is more anxious to do work in that particular area than to accomplish your objectives.

Again, request references of clients in circumstances similar to yours. Specify that you want the names of clients the advisor has served for at least three years.

Ask questions about the advisor's background and education, services, compensation, and regulatory compliance. The background and education of financial advisors can vary as much as the services they offer. An advisor's education and experience should illustrate a solid foundation in fiscal planning and a commitment to keeping current.

Financial advisors provide an array of services. Make sure they match your needs. Costs include the fees and commissions you pay. A complete comparison between advisors will require full information about all possible total costs. You should have this information before entering into any agreement.

In most circumstances, the SEC requires registration of individuals or firms offering the public financial planning services. Remember to check to make sure the advisor you are considering is registered.

CHAPTER 9

Calculating Risk, Overcoming Fear

The late Amos Tversky was a Stanford University psychologist who studied people's feelings about risk. He found that the perception of risk is nonsymmetrical: most people worry more about *not losing money* than they do about making it.

I remember playing golf with my father one day forty years ago, during which we spent three or four holes arguing about the outcome of a coin flip. Although my father was a lawyer, he had worked his way through college playing pool and poker, so he was fluent with statistics, although his tended to be applied (or gamblers') statistics.

On this occasion, my father took the point of view that if you were to flip a coin and show eight heads in a row, chances were that the next coin flip would come up tails. Or, if you were to have eight tails in a row, the next coin would come up heads. Scientifically, this is completely wrong. The coin is not aware of what it did on the last flip, so with each new flip the odds of heads or tails are always the same: fifty-fifty.

The stock market works the same way. If you ask a statistician what the odds are of a 10 percent increase or a 10 percent decrease in the market over, say, the next six months, he or she would claim that the odds for both are exactly the same. To a statistician, being down 20 percent when the market is down 30 percent is equivalent to being up 30 percent when the market is up 20 percent. In both instances, you're plus ten.

However, if you ask most investors what they think of such reasoning, they will tell you that they don't want any part of it. If the market goes down 30 percent and some investor's portfolio only goes down 20 percent, that investor will never say, "Hey, we are doing great. We were only down 20 percent." The average investor just doesn't think that way—which makes me a little nervous about a financial arrangement we made with one of our clients two years ago.

The client wanted to be prepared for the next bear market. So when we signed the contract, he said, "What we want to do is reward you if you beat the bogie." (The bogie in this case being market indices, such as the S&P 500 or the Dow Jones.) "It doesn't matter if the market is down 25 percent. If you are only down 20 percent, you are plus five percent and we would love to pay you for that difference."

I know the client believes he will still want to pay even in a bear market, but psychologically it will be a lot tougher than he thinks. When people are losing money, they don't like the idea of rewarding someone just because the money lost was less than the market index. I have tried to tell this client, "You are going to hate paying me if the market goes down. You are going to do everything you can to break that contract. You are not going to want to pay us the difference." His response is, "Oh yeah, we really will, no problem."

So far, the issue has been entirely academic, because the market hasn't gone down, let alone sharply. Eventually it will, and when it does, I know he's going to hate paying us. Anyone who pays off gladly when he's losing money is very different than most people who invest in the market.

Cycle of Fear and Greed

Most investors don't have any coherent investment strategy in a declining market. When a stock starts to fall, they can't bear to sell at a loss; when they finally do decide to take action, it's usually at the wrong time (see Figure 9.1).

Typically, if an investor has bought a stock at 30 and the price suddenly goes to 25, our investor doesn't sell, because he or she doesn't want to absorb that $5 per share loss. So he declares compromise: "I'll sell at 28."

The stock goes up to 27, never quite reaches 28, then turns around and drops to 20. Now the investor has to reevaluate his position: "I've learned my lesson. I'll sell at 25." Except the stock never gets to 25. It only gets to 24. While he's waiting, the stock drops to 15. This time the investor says, "I'll sell at 20." But the stock never gets that high either. Instead it falls all the way to 15.

The investor can't bear the thought of selling at 15 and taking a $15 per share loss. So to maintain a little dignity, he decides to sell only when the stock hits 18. The stock bounces around, and this time—miracle of miracles—it actually does get up to 18, whereupon the investor sells everything. By now you can no doubt guess the rest of the story—over the next couple of months the stock goes all the way to 50.

Moral of the story: Unless you have both a theory of investing that makes sense and the personal discipline to stick

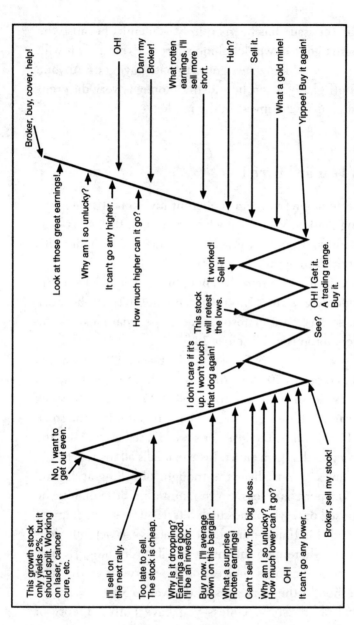

SOURCE: Anonymous

Figure 9.1   The Cycle of Fear and Greed

to it, the market will chew you to bits. Because nothing is ever clear-cut in the market (there's usually more varying shades of gray than clear black-and-white), I am surprised that people don't take more nuanced approaches. When I go to a cocktail party with investors, all the talk is on binary issues: "Did you own it or not?" "I had it when it was hot." Well, the fact that you owned a hot stock doesn't mean anything. The issue is how much you owned. A couple of shares doesn't mean anything; you wouldn't be able to see what impact it had on your portfolio if you did the calculation out to eight decimal places. The important thing is not *whether* you owned a stock but *how much* you owned and what the average purchase price was.

When we buy a stock, we are almost certain it isn't at the lowest relative price. If it were, we would buy the whole position right there. Of much more concern to us is our average purchase price, our average sales price, the yield, and total return.

Extrapolating to Oblivion

In the short run, you can't predict the market and it's useless to try. You certainly can't look at recent trends and make a prediction. People are very selective about what time periods they choose to look at when extrapolating a trend. Typically they start with a peak, go to a trough, and extrapolate down to oblivion. Either that or they do the reverse—start with a trough, go to a peak, and extrapolate up to infinity.

Reality is far less volatile than the typical investor's perception of it. A trend isn't trough-to-peak or peak-to-trough. A trend is peak-to-peak or trough-to-trough. In short, it's a channel, not a line. The reason people make such drastic mistakes about their portfolio, the market, or a specific stock is that they look at last week, last quarter, or last year and then conclude that it was a close approximation to normal.

What they should be looking at is the last twenty, thirty, or forty years. That's normal—not the last month, the last three months, or the last year. If you want a general rule, assume that major market troughs are five to six years apart and that on average markets will rise for three or four years, then decline for two or three years.

Normal is average. That's what you look for. We have had a bull market ever since August of 1982. The Dow started at 720. By 1997, it was over 6700. That's more than an 800 percent increase. Will the Dow increase an additional 800 percent over the next fourteen years? No.

What we will probably see is a return to historic averages. You can't forecast from a high, which is what we had in the late sixties, and say we are going to have a 10 percent return forever, because that's not what happens. In this business, you can't extrapolate. You can't measure trends from peak-to-trough and trough-to-peak, because you end up with stocks that vanish entirely or grow forever, and that isn't what happens in real life. In real life momentum buyers drive a stock up and up and up until its price is totally indefensible, at which point everybody suddenly realizes it and the stock falls off a cliff. The same thing happens when the market is driving a stock price down. Psychologists have a name for this kind of behavior—they call it the submissive dog syndrome.

Submissive Dogs and the Binary Flip

Most of the time, cheap stocks (like expensive stocks) revert to the mean. But as long as stocks are at extremes they are dangerous. If a cheap stock has been down a long time, the dispersion of return becomes very great. At some point you end up with a binary condition: maybe it's going into bankruptcy or maybe it is going to be a big winner; either the company exists or it does not.

The stock is acting like a submissive dog. Dogs, when you back them into a corner, tend to become more and more submissive—but only up to a point. Eventually the dog totally flips and becomes a very aggressive dog.

The stock market works similarly. When looking at the history of a stock you can't just extrapolate events either to catastrophe or to infinity and say whatever is currently going on will continue on forever. Sooner or later the stock (the submissive dog) will turn on you.

It's hard to say what causes stocks to suddenly change direction. A stock whose price is falling might be falling for a very good reason—the company is about to go bankrupt. But what about a stock that's continually going up? When a stock continues to go up month after month, people who own that stock become not only accustomed to unbroken price rises, they see them as inevitable. Then when the eventual day of reckoning comes—the company gets hit with a bad quarter— the stockholders suddenly snap back to reality, realize they'd been swept away by the mania of the day, and liquidate their positions.

Inflation in the economy can cause a similar kind of problem. Normally, inflation is bad for the economy, but just a little inflation might not be all that bad. In the short run, it often seems to have no effect on the market at all. Then you get slightly higher inflation and slightly higher interest rates. Nothing happens. No impact at all. You may be lulled into thinking that inflation will never have an impact. Well, if you keep on doing this, eventually you end up with a stock that's like a dog in a corner—suddenly it turns on you, and the market collapses.

When I was an investment trainee, I was taught a rule that seemed carved in stone: the PE should be 17 and inflation and interest rates don't matter. At most you have a little variation around 17. If you get up to a PE of 20, that's too expensive. If you have a PE of 15, that's really cheap. But the average is 17, and if inflation and interest rates are moving up, don't worry about it; they have no impact. That's what we were taught.

However, what happens in real life is that there always comes a point when interest rates and inflation move up and—wham!—suddenly you reach a tipping point where all the effects take place at once (there's that submissive dog again).

The Plaintive Cry of the Defensive Manager

By the summer of 1996, the market had been going up virtually in a straight line for fourteen years. At SKB&A, our clients were getting rich. As so-called "value managers," we weren't doing quite as well as some other managers, but we weren't doing badly; more importantly, we were doing it at lower risk. Even so, some clients were not impressed. In the middle of giant bull markets like the one that started in 1982, there are always going to be some clients who don't want to hear about less-than-market volatility—we don't get any credit for that. What they want to see is high appreciation. Then you get sudden drops (like the great correction of October 1987), and suddenly everyone remembers why they hired a defensive management firm in the first place.

I'm not saying we don't go down in bear markets. Sometimes we go down the same as everyone else. We just go down a lot less. But since we haven't had a bear market in fourteen years, people are less likely to care about investors who do better in market declines or in slow advances. We just plod along doing boring stuff—buying cheap stocks, skipping over expensive stocks, not paying any attention to today's fads, and not even providing much of anything for clients to talk about at cocktail parties.

Our defensive strategy really proved itself in October 1987, when the market went from 2700 to 1700 in less than two months, including a drop of 500 points in a single day. Some financial reporters completely panicked. The *Wall Street Journal* quoted one well-known newsletter writer as saying this was going to be the worst financial shakeout since the industrial revolution. Another thought it meant at least a recession and possibly a full-scale depression.

At the time, I was still with the Bank of California. One of my clients called and asked, "Will I be able to eat tomorrow?" It was really quite touching. She was eighty years old and had lived through the Great Depression, and it had made a strong impression. Now she had around $3.5 million, and at her age didn't have time to recover if she lost everything a second time. So when she called right after the Monday crash, I told her not to worry.

"I'm taking care of you," I said. "We have a balanced portfolio. We own treasury securities. This is exactly why we own treasury securities. We don't believe this is the beginning of another depression. But we have benchmarks set out just in case and we will be watching those closely for the next two to three months."

I wasn't just blowing a lot of smoke. We had been expecting something like this for some time—not a 500-point drop in one day, but we knew the market was edging toward a correction of some sort. Back in late June I had written a memo arguing that we could very well see a 150-point, one-day drop in the market.

In a situation like this, you want to own some bonds for protection. The question was, what kind of bonds? Long-term treasury bonds were a good deal in the summer of 1987, offering 9½ percent yield, which to us was just totally out-of-line cheap, because when you do the add-ons for risk, you end up with higher inflation reflected in that yield than we thought likely. If bonds weren't cheap at 9½ percent then stocks were incredibly overvalued. It was just too much of a disparity. When the market crashed in October, our holdings in treasury bonds protected most of our clients—during the fourth quarter of 1987, we made almost as much on our bond portfolios as we lost on stocks.

In November we had our annual meeting with the family of the little old lady who had been worrying about having enough money to eat. Whereas the market had gone down 37 percent between August and October, this woman, who owned cheap stocks and long-term treasury bonds, had an account that was only down 5 percent.

I don't claim all the credit for this. There are some clients who will invariably do the wrong things at the wrong time. This woman was not one of those. The reason she had $3.5 million to invest was that she was a true long-term investor. She had been a client of ours since the late seventies. Her husband had built his wealth from the mid-thirties, so she was never a skittish type. Except for the Great Depression, she'd had good experiences with her investments. She was sophisticated enough not to particularly care if the market dropped. She just wanted to be sure this wasn't a replay of the Crash of 1929.

Although I hadn't really been aware that her portfolio was only down 5 percent when I'd talked to her on the phone, I knew her portfolio was a diversified one. I knew what treasury securities had done—rates had gone from 9.5 percent to 8 percent in a very short time and prices had gone up a lot. Since I didn't have knowledge of her precise numbers at the time, you might argue, I suppose, that I was giving her more hope than the circumstances warranted. On the other hand, even if I didn't have the actual numbers, I knew I was in the ballpark—sometimes you have to keep clients comfortable so they don't do bad things to their investments and, subsequently, themselves.

The Capital Market Pricing Model: Risk Equals Reward

Because we always take our risks in stocks, not bonds, the correction of 1987 really didn't hurt us much. People who owned junk bonds, on the other hand, got pretty badly battered. If you are going to invest in anything other than treasury securities, you want to be really highly paid. You know treasury bonds are safe because whatever else happens, the U.S. government is going to repay its debts.

Because treasury bonds are the lowest risk security, most of the time they trade as such. Any time treasury securities start selling at a higher yield than triple-A bonds, watch out. The U.S. government will do whatever it takes to make sure it has superior credit to any corporation. Normally there is a regular downward progression in credit quality from treasuries to triple-A to double-A bonds. Whenever that's not true the government will use its power—including its power to tax—to make sure the trend doesn't continue.

Investors in the early 1980s thought they had the system beat because they could get 18 percent on ninety-day treasury bills. That's something you don't see every day—the lowest risk security offering the highest rate of return. Of course, it didn't last. The rates quickly went from 18 to 16 to 12 to 10 to 8 to 6 to 4 to an eventual low of 2½ percent. Since then, they have returned to 4 or 5 percent.

In the long run financial markets always obey the odds. For a while you can go to Las Vegas and beat the craps table, but Vegas was not built by letting the clients win. You can't beat City Hall and you can't beat the house, and the federal government has the biggest house. Sure, its bonds can become worthless, but by God it is going to take down everything else before it. That's how the Capital Market Pricing Model works. The more risk you take, the greater your reward. You occasionally get abnormalities in the short term, but in the long run everything reverts to the mean.

There was a time in the late 1980s when it looked like the more risk you took with stocks the lower your returns were. All that meant was that either low-risk stocks were overvalued or higher-risk stocks were undervalued. Such things don't last. The Capital Market Pricing Model works. It merely says that the rate of return of ninety-day T-bills is going to be lower than the rate of return on the S&P 500 in the long run and that thirty-year treasury bonds fall in between.

I have to believe in the Capital Market Pricing Model. It's the basis on which the whole economic system works. Occasionally stocks can get so high in value that their return gets depressed for a couple of years. But what is a couple of years? Eventually the S&P 500 will correct its overvaluation. Either there will be a sharp decline in the market, over the slow passing of time or some combination of the two. But sooner or later the market catches up with reality.

Bear Market Jitters

Last spring, the market dropped again, and one of my individual clients called: "We have to meet with you."

I told him I didn't think he really had to go to all that trouble. He said, "We're going to be in San Francisco next week anyway." This was on a Thursday. On Friday the market went up. Over the weekend I ran into him at a birthday party. He said, "Aw, don't worry about it." He had just had a temporary case of the jitters. I didn't blame him. It was his money. He had a right to be concerned.

It's hard to know what will happen if we hit an extended decline today. I like to think that my individual clients are self-selected, they are smart, they know exactly what they bought when they hired us, they are in for the long term, and they aren't going to panic in a decline. But we haven't had a bear market in a long time. The year 1987 caught everyone's attention, even though it only lasted a short while and overall the market was up in 1987. In fact, 1990 was the only year of market index decline in nearly fifteen years.

My oldest son is thirty-one. He's bright, clear thinking, and well informed. Will a bear market scare him? Well, I have thirty years of experience in the investment business, and bear markets still scare me. I'd be very surprised if they didn't scare him too. During the first half of his life nothing happened in the market at all. Ever since he was in high school he's seen nothing but a bull market. What does he or any other young person know about bear markets? At the Fidelity Funds group, for example, the portfolio managers are mostly in their late twenties or early thirties (I don't mean to single Fidelity out; it's the same everywhere).

When the current bull market started back in 1982, many of the current managers were still in high school. They don't have any experience with anything before that. How can you talk to them about the bear market of 1973–74, which took place when most of them were in the third grade? If you try to tell them about the way the market was back in 1962 (when I was in business school), you might as well be talking about the War of 1812. Some of these young portfolio managers have led such a charmed life when it comes to market declines that they look back on 1987 as a bear market (even though the market actually went up that year). Their attitude is: "I've seen bear markets. They're no big thing."

Even if they do go back twenty years and look at the market they still won't get a true picture. In 1975 the market was just coming out of the 1973–74 decline. If you look forward from then to the present, the numbers look spectacular. I mean, when you start at the bottom and go up from there, what else can the numbers be but great? At the end of 1975 the market was 700 or 800. By the beginning of 1997 it was 6700. The twenty-year rates of return were astonishing.

When these young people see a real drop, they'll probably think it's the end of the world. They'll be talking like it's 1924 Germany, where people walked around with bushel baskets full of money. Well, the reason everyone keeps looking for 1924 Germany again is that it was an anomaly. The next bear market won't be any more the end of the world than it was in 1974 or in 1932 or at any other point in time. Some people don't understand that the market wobbles here and wobbles there and even crashes from time to time.

There's only one way to deal with a bear market and that's to decide what you're going to do before you ever get into one. The last thing you want to be doing is trying to make rational decisions when the market is either going through the roof and everyone is manic, thinking it's never going to stop, or the market is crashing and everyone is walking around with butter-flies in their stomachs and fear in their eyes.

In 1926, smart people were saying the market was getting dangerous, and they were right. Unfortunately, anyone who said that didn't have any clients by 1929. The really smart people were the ones who said, "The market is over-valued," and got out in 1928. By the time they got to 1929, no one was saying the market was overpriced anymore. They were all caught up in it. Everything was too crazed.

Really good thinking never comes at the end of a bull market anyway. In the 1929 crash, all the clear-headed thinking really came the year before, when people had the leisure to be thoughtful and methodical: "Are we overvalued, under-valued, or about right?" When you are in the middle of a cri-sis, it is hard to think rationally.

Preparing for the Downturn

When an investment company gets hit with an unexpected bear market, its first reaction is to panic and its second (equally useless) reaction is to commission a study. There's nothing wrong with doing studies, if they are done before a market decline. But if a company waits until we're in the middle of a bear market to start a six- to nine-month study, it'll probably miss the bear market entirely. Furthermore, by doing a study in the middle of a crisis it'll focus on the wrong area. The investment company will be worrying about what it owns, because what it owns will undoubtedly be expensive stocks.

If the company had bought cheap stocks, it wouldn't be worrying nearly as much. When a cheap stock goes down it only becomes a bigger bargain. A real expensive stock can go down and still be expensive.

I'm not saying that just because a stock goes up it's expensive and just because it goes down it's cheap. You have to ask, "Where did the stock start from?" If it started from very cheap and it goes up, it still might be cheap. If it started from very expensive and it declined, it may still be expensive.

The Great Correction

Because I'd been looking for a 150-point, one-day market correction for the previous three months, when the market did finally drop 500 points on October 19, 1987, I was surprised but not panicked. As calls from worried clients came in, I told them I didn't think it was the end of the world, but just in case we were watching for it.

The real concern in any market decline is deflation. Between 1929 and 1932, deflation led to lowered demand, falling prices, and expenses out of line with revenues. So businesses reduced expenses and laid off workers, which reduced demand even further. Pretty soon the whole economy was chasing its tail.

The government stepped in too, increasing taxes to satisfy Wall Street that the government was doing something and passing the Smoot-Hawley tariff bill to protect American industry. Once the economy hit bottom, other government programs made the Depression so much worse that it took the stock market 25 years to reach its 1929 peaks again.

In contrast, in the aftermath of the correction of 1987, Ronald Reagan did nothing at all—no Oval Office speeches, no reassurances about having nothing to fear but fear itself, and no lectures on malaise. As a result, the correction of 1987 was nothing more than a minor blip in what now is a fourteen-year-old bull market.

However, since we didn't know any of this on October 20, 1987, we did the prudent thing after a 500-point drop and set out benchmarks for internationally traded industrial commodities. If we were going to have a deflationary depression, we wanted to know about it right away. And one of the first things that happens in a depression is that commodity prices drop.

When I mention commodities, you might think of agricultural commodities: cattle, wheat, corn, soybeans. The problem is that they go up and down all the time. It's all meaningless noise. What you need are indicators that represent basic necessities, aren't subject to local fluctuations, and are traded around the world. We came up with four global industrial commodities: copper, silver, gold, and lumber.

In the Great Depression of 1929 to 1932, these commodities all went down, including gold. After the big drop of October 1987, however, we could tell our clients with confidence that no depression was coming—when we looked at the numbers, deflationary pressures just weren't there. The price of lumber went up. Copper didn't go below fifty-five cents, which is where its bottom had been before. Gold went up and down, but we didn't see the abyss. In short, not only were prices not falling off cliffs, they were hardly changing at all.

One reason: this 500-point drop wasn't quite what it initially seemed. The market had not been going along on some solid plateau from which it suddenly fell 500 points in one day. The market had been shooting upward prior to the crash. I had written something about it in early July—Independence Day was on my mind—called "Elliot Rides a Rocket," which is how most people were looking at the market in the summer of 1987. On the Fourth of July, the market was going up like a skyrocket. It was all fireworks. Most people didn't treat it as anything more than a flash, a burst—something that was not substantial.

Of course the market was bound to come back down. It was nothing more than the inevitable consequence of its having gone up so fast in the first place. Fireworks go up; they explode; they come down. And that was what October 1987 really was. The market went from 2100 up to 2750, came down to 1750, bounced back up two days later to 1900, and then by the following February was back up to 2200.

At the time, some people were saying, "Uh-oh, this is going to have a big impact on retail sales. Earnings will go straight into the toilet and the economy will spiral down the tubes." But if the market had no positive impact on retail sales when it was going up earlier in the summer, why would it have a negative impact when it went back down in October? Now, could it have? Sure. That's why we set out the commodity benchmarks in the first place. What was the net effect on the economy? There wasn't any.

You Can't Fire Debt

Deflation is pernicious. It initially leads to lower volume and immediately thereafter to lower prices on the lower volume. The revenues end up in the tank, and if a company lags in cutting expenses or laying off workers, its earnings disappear. That is particularly true of companies that fire people during a resizing, then spend a lot of money on equipment to improve productivity. Productivity is terrific in a rising economy, but when the economy goes south a company can end up with a lot of fixed capital costs. There is a big difference between capital expenses and labor. One can lay off employees, but one can't fire debt or the interest on debt, just as one can't fire a computer or a pump.

Back in the sixties, when I followed the machinery industry, numerically controlled machine tools were a brand-new technology. Some analysts were arguing that this new technology was incredibly productive, which would guarantee high profitability for the manufacturers; they were convinced that these companies' stocks would be sure-fire winners for the next ten or fifteen years.

At first glance, this argument seemed to make sense. By the mid-sixties, most machine tools dated from World War II, which is to say they were already twenty to twenty-five years old. The new numerically controlled machines were far more productive—one numerically controlled machine tool operated by two people could do the work of four lathes and four lathe operators.

Fortunately, our firm wasn't convinced. We said, "Wait a minute. Each company that buys a numerically controlled machine tool will have two less people to fire if the country goes into recession."

In our view, it didn't make sense to buy as many of the new machine tools as some of the more optimistic analysts wanted these companies to, no matter how productive they were. In addition, the companies said, "Our flexibility will be lost if we replace our old machines with numerically controlled machine tools. We've already depreciated all of our current machine tools. So all we have is the variable cost of the labor."

Not all companies saw it this way, however. Some thought the smart thing to do was to fire their older workers, buy new machine tools, and increase productivity.

From a short-term, bottom-line point of view, this line of thinking seems to make sense. Three or four years ago the expectation was that profitability in the economy would remain crummy forever. That was when some companies totally embraced downsizing, resizing, and that whole mean-and-lean thought process. These companies pushed for productivity, bought expensive new capital equipment, and relentlessly laid off workers. Companies can do this for a while, especially if expenses are no higher than projections and revenues are better. And with a high level of operating leverage from capital expenditures rather than people, profitability will pop right up, because expenses are fixed.

The problem for these companies comes when they suddenly run into the next economic slowdown. Their revenues won't meet budget; they'll still have that high fixed cost; since they didn't hire anyone, they won't have anyone to fire; they'll have no flexibility. Their earnings will end up in the tank.

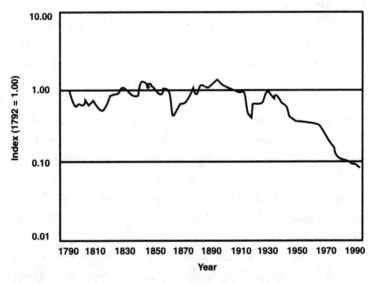

SOURCE: American Institute for Economic Research: Great Barrington, Massachusetts

Figure 9.2   Purchasing Power of the U.S. Dollar, 1792 to 1996

Table 9.1   Inflation's Effect on Value of U.S. Dollar

Inflation Rate	Years to Halve the Value of $1.00
2.0%	36
3.0%	24
4.0%	18

The Danger of Inflation

Inflation is probably the most critical and ignored issue in planning. Even though its effects can be dramatic, most people underestimate how rapidly high inflation rates can erode the value of their real assets.

For most of U.S. history, the purchasing power of the dollar has held steady (see Figures 9.2 and 9.3). Although inflation increased during the war years, once the wars were over deflation restored the dollar's purchasing power. Since World War II, however, inflationary periods have not been followed by periods of restoration. Partly this is a result of political decisions and partly it comes from going off the gold standard in the mid-sixties and closing the gold window in 1972.

Although many people ignore them, inflation assumptions make a very large difference in the rate of decline in purchasing power. Currently, most consumers believe that the future inflation rate will be in the 2 percent to 4 percent range. While this seems like a fairly narrow range, whether it is 2 percent or 4 percent will make a big difference in the number of years it takes to cut purchasing power in half (see Table 9.1).

An easy way to calculate doubling effects (or 50 percent decreases) is to use the Rule of Seventy-Two, shown in Table 9.2. For example, if the rate of return on an asset is 6 percent,

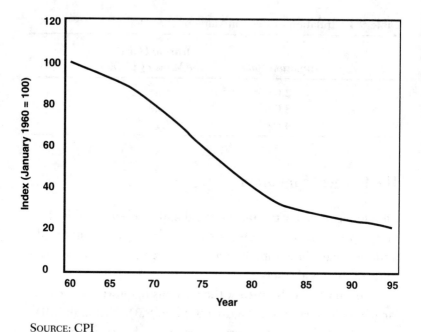

SOURCE: CPI

Figure 9.3   *Purchasing Power of the U.S. Dollar, Since 1960*

it will take twelve years to double the asset's value (72/6 = 12); if you want to double your assets in five years, you must achieve a 14.4 percent annual return. At an 8 percent inflation rate, the purchasing power of the currency will be cut in half in nine years. At a 6 percent inflation rate, it will be cut in half in twelve years. At a 3 percent inflation rate, purchasing power will be cut in half in twenty-four years. At a 2 percent inflation rate, it will be cut in half in thirty-six years.

While a 0 percent to 1 percent range is clearly preferable, reaching this range would require creating policies that give people the power to decide how to spend their own

Table 9.2 The Rule of Seventy-Two

Compounding/ Discount Rate	Number of Years to Double
0.5%	144.0
1.0%	72.0
1.5%	48.0
2.0%	36.0
2.5%	28.8
3.0%	24.0
3.5%	20.6
4.0%	18.0
4.5%	16.0
5.0%	14.4
5.5%	13.1
6.0%	12.0
6.5%	11.1
7.0%	10.3
7.5%	9.6
8.0%	9.0
8.5%	8.5
9.0%	8.0

money. Lower tax rates and reduced federal government programs are the only way to get both higher growth and lower inflation, but it will take an angry and aroused middle class to do it. Only the middle 80 percent of the population understands that a 3 percent wage gain canceled out by a 3 percent inflation rate destroys their ability to save any money, either for retirement or anything else.

CHAPTER 10

Your Last Chance

There are some people who would never want me as their investment advisor, and there are some people I would never want as a client. I certainly wouldn't want someone who demands the highest returns all the time—every month, every quarter—and isn't satisfied with anything less than 30 percent a year. That's an irrational expectation and it would require our company to take far more risk than we think is appropriate.

This isn't a rare occurrence. Most investors take more risk for less return than necessary, because they like to have something to chat about at cocktail parties ("What do you own? What do you think is really going on?").

When someone says he or she wants to make 35 percent to 50 percent a year, I reply, "Terrific! Go see a venture capitalist; buy a company; concentrate all your ownership in one stock. We can't help you. We practice diversification and risk sanity."

Our company takes the point of view that if we have to take off-the-chart risks to achieve a given rate of return, we won't make the investment. The first thing I do when I talk to a prospective client is find out how reasonable he or she is. Some people we never want as clients because they have such unreasonably high expectations; no matter how well we do for them, they're never happy. I don't even want to deal with these kinds of people. Why play a game where the best we can do is zero?

Let's say someone comes into our firm and says, "Okay, I understand risk. What can you do for me?" This is a person we can at least work with. Next, we need to know what percentage of total assets the client intends to entrust to us. If this person owns his or her own company and does nothing but roll over short-maturity municipal bonds because he or she is already taking a lot of risk with the company, then we can't be of help. These kinds of people tend to be heavy-duty, risk-taking entrepreneurs. After they die, their spouses and their kids might be terrific prospects, but these kinds of entrepreneurs are not. They have different definitions of risk than we do. If it's their project and they're in charge, they don't consider the situation risky at all. An advisor can't win in these situations, because these people don't think rationally about risk. Why collect a fee if we can't do anything for them? When we encounter someone like that, we say, "Terrific, when you sell your company we'd love to have you as a client."

If on the other hand the client is rational about risk and expected returns, we next want to know his or her tolerance for risk. There is a vast difference between one client with a ninety-eight-year-old aunt on her deathbed about to leave $10 million and another client with no wealthy relatives anywhere. These are two totally different situations, and not because one account is $10 million bigger than the other. The wealthy client can tolerate far more risk than the other, but still might not want to take it.

I also need to know the client's personal attitudes about money. I once had a client whose uncle had just died and left him $1 million. He didn't know his uncle had a million dollars. It was such a big shock; it made him feel guilty. He initially thought that this money had to be treated differently than his other assets, since it wasn't something he had earned. It had been given to him. He felt he had a special responsibility toward it. It had to be protected.

Six months later, his attitude had undergone a dramatic change. He said, "It is my money and I am going to use it." He began to spend some of it, which is fine. His uncle did not specify that he become a steward of this money for future generations or that he should use it only to improve mankind. Money is money. Only the client's attitude toward it was different. Over time, his attitude changed, and now he doesn't differentiate—as he shouldn't—between his own money and the money he inherited.

No two people react the same way to a sudden windfall. Take two seemingly identical clients—same age, same job, same income, and each one inherits $10 million. One client might say, "Gee, $10 million, that is more than my family is ever going to need, for God's sake be careful what you do with it." The other client, in contrast, might very well say, "Well, you know, $10 million is a lot of money but $5 million is also a lot of money. Let's go for it. Let's try to make it $50 million."

Risk Versus Age

It's not true that some people are born financially reckless and others are cautious all their lives. People go through cycles. Their attitudes toward money change over time.

I don't think today's thirty-year-old investors are more courageous than I was at age thirty; human nature hasn't changed that much in twenty-five years. During a 10 percent market decline, a thirty-year-old investor may panic more than a fifty-year-old investor. On the other hand, a seventy-year-old person may panic as much as the thirty-year-old person despite age, experience, and maturity.

Why?

He or she has more to lose and less time to earn it back.

A person's ability to take risks is not an inverse function of age, which is to say it's not a smooth, straight decline. There are peaks and valleys. It is an interrelationship of liabilities, asset growth, and income fluctuations. No single answer applies to everyone.

In my case, I am fifty-seven years old. My liability stream has peaked. I don't have a kid in college anymore. I have a house and a second house for weekends. That's it. My income is still going up. My maximum tolerance for risk will probably be at its highest for the next ten years.

At age twenty or twenty-five, I had huge risk-taking ability too, but I didn't have any money to take advantage of it. For most people, the years between thirty and fifty bring multiple liabilities. They get married, buy a house, have children, plan for college expenses. They really can't afford a lot of risk.

Now I am at a point in my life where I can take more risk, because if something goes wrong, at age fifty-seven I still have time to earn it back. I expect to live long enough to see one more giant bull market, which is to say, a period of a three- to fivefold increase in value. I've already had one bull market in my investment career, from 1982 till today. Typically, a person gets two. People who start early enough and live long enough maybe get three.

If you are at age fifty now, in good health, and earning a decent income, then these are probably your best years for putting together the portfolio you'll need for your retirement. This may, in fact, be your last chance.

Think Before You Plunge

Given today's market peaks, one thing you don't want to do is have as much in stocks today as you had fifteen years ago before the market went up fivefold. If it was right for you to have 55 percent of your assets in stock at the start of this bull market, it can't be right today for you to have 75 percent or 85 percent in stocks. It doesn't make sense—you're fifteen years older. Even if you argue that you can take more risk today because you're at your peak earning years, you still have to calculate how much.

This gets you into what kinds of returns are reasonable on different stocks and different stock groups. Knowing that a stock did better than the market in the past doesn't mean it is going to continue to do better in the future. You can't measure a trend from a trough to a peak and extrapolate the stock up forever. Eventually you'll have reversion toward the mean.

If you have had a crummy below-average year, it's likely that the following year will be pretty good; if you have had a great year, it is likely that the following year won't be so hot. These are averages, not rules. Over time you will see much more averaging out and much more smoothing.

Because many investors really don't understand regression toward the mean, we often have to take steps to protect clients from themselves. Some people wouldn't take any risk at all, which isn't smart. Other people are plungers who would take everything they own and plunk it down on one particularly beloved stock, which isn't smart either.

In most cases, it's not difficult to talk people out of going to extremes. I just point out the negative consequences of either taking no risk or taking too much risk, and the clients come to the right conclusions by themselves. The problem is that a lot of people act before they think. What we need to do is slow them down and ask if they're sure that's what they want to do.

If they still say they want to do it, then terrific—it's their money and their right. But if they say, "Gee, maybe not," then perhaps we've done them a service.

Three-Year Projections

Over the last seventy years, stocks have returned much more than long-term treasury bonds. The question then arises: Why invest in bonds at all? If you have twenty-five, fifty, or seventy years to invest, then there is no good reason, especially if the total rate of return on stocks is 10 percent or more a year.

But suppose you have a much shorter horizon. The fact that stocks have returned an average of 10 percent a year over seventy years says nothing about what stocks will do *next* year or in the next ten years.

When I started in this business in 1965, if I had said to myself, "The market goes up 10 percent a year. I want to own stocks," what I would have found was that over the next seventeen years the market hadn't changed at all. There was no appreciation. Dividend income averaged about 5 percent, or about half the total return normally generated by stocks over a seventy-year period.

That was thirty years ago. What about today? It's not a bad forecast to assume a 10 percent return on stocks for the next seventy years, but for the next one to five years, it's not good at all. The historic standard deviation that goes with that 10 percent return is currently around 17 percent. If you make a forecast for the next year based on those long-term numbers, your rate of return will most likely be 10 percent *plus or minus 17*. That gives you a range anywhere from plus 27 percent to minus 7 percent.

Is that what it is going to fall into?

Possibly.

But it could also be *two* standard deviations down, which is just plain spooky.

One thing to remember: we usually don't get three super years in a row. In 1995, the market had a plus 37 percent rate of return. For 1996, the total return on the S&P 500 was about 23 percent, but back in 1994 we only had a 1.5 percent return.

Here's a handy rule of thumb: If the first year was great, the second year will tend to be merely okay, and the third year can easily be negative. So if 1995 was great, and 1996 was pretty good, then 1997 might be average to pretty poor.

Know When to Be Timid and When to Be Aggressive

When it comes to dealing with pension fund managers, some CEOs have a blind spot. Because they know what it is like to be regularly criticized for their quarterly results by people who don't understand their long-term strategy, when they go to pick a manager for the company's pension fund, they go out of their way to find people with a long-term view and the ability to ignore short-term noise. Still, in spite of all this, the next time they meet with the manager to discuss the fund, the first thing they say is, "What happened last week?"

When I was at the Bank of California, we ran the pension plan for a forklift manufacturer. It happened to be a highly cyclical company. When its sales were good, its profits were terrific. When sales were not good, profits were horrible. This isn't unusual for manufacturers of big-ticket items, but it caused the company to bounce back and forth between extreme prosperity and deep despair—"We are never going to sell another forklift again."

An investor had to take a long-term view to own this company's stock, especially since management compounded the company's cyclical nature by arguing that it was an aggressive company and therefore wanted investment managers that were aggressive too. I told them, "What you really need is a counterbalance. Your earnings are going all over the place. They're not forecastable. They're highly cyclical. Use your pension plan for a counterbalance."

If management had been smarter, it would have decided to fund future benefits by doubling or tripling contributions to the pension plan when times were plush, then slowing down when business was bad. Given the extremely cyclical nature of the forklift business, management should have hired managers who did well when business was down and didn't do as well when business was going great. However, the management insisted that it was a very aggressive company, and it wanted everything and everyone to be aggressive.

An aggressive company, run by aggressive managers, out for the most aggressive returns. But what did the company do when push came to shove? It fired all its pension plan managers and bought annuities—the most conservative, risk-free, low-returning investment it could find. Under the circumstances, buying annuities was about as wishy-washy a way as one could find.

"How Do I Double My Money in a Year?"

When people are young, they really should make a big commitment in high-growth stocks. But because of the liabilities of family and home staring them in the face, most people tend to be very conservative, and that's not the best thing. They postpone making a decision for one month, and then the months go into years and the years go into decades.

What you want is long periods of high growth even though you may be hitting some volatility in between. You can take the volatility when you are thirty years old, because by the time you are seventy years old you won't even remember it.

In the bear market of 1973–74, the Dow went from something over 1000 to about 500, but it quickly rebounded, and by the beginning of 1997 the Dow was 6700. Measuring the gain from peak to peak, the market went from 1000 to 6700. That early drop from 1000 to 500, which seemed like such a disaster at the time, doesn't even show up.

High liabilities make people conservative, so they go out and buy insurance policies or guaranteed investment contracts, which is a mistake. Because they have plenty of time to bail themselves out, they really should go for aggressive growth. Time will make the kind of volatility that seems so excruciating in the short run virtually disappear in the long run.

In my experience, people don't take enough risk when they are under thirty years of age. They may get the risk right when they are aged thirty to fifty, but then they don't take enough risk again when they are aged fifty to seventy. Then there are some people who come into the office at age sixty-nine, planning to retire at age seventy, and say, "Holy cow, I don't have enough money to live on. I am going to retire next year. I need to know how to double my money in a year." "Forget it," I tell them. "It's too late. Learn to live on less."

High Marginal Tax Rates and the Older Investor

One big problem with government tax policy is that just as people reach retirement age, where they should be taking less risk, high capital gains tax rates push them into taking more. There's a huge difference between selling securities when you have no tax impact and selling securities when you have to pay 35 percent.

In many instances, elderly people have owned their stocks for twenty or thirty years. What was right for them when they were in their fifties isn't anywhere near right for them now that they are in their seventies. But their imbedded costs (their cost basis) is so low and their capital gains bracket is so high that they own either too much of one kind of stock or too much stock in general. If they die and leave the stock to their children, then their children don't have to pay capital gains; but if the parents sell the stock before they die, they take a huge financial hit, even though at their age it may not be appropriate for them to own so much stock.

This is a terrible way to allocate resources. You end up with people who sit there and say, "I'd rather die than give the government my money!" And by God they will. That money will just sit there even though it may not be appropriate, either by percentage or type stock. In situations like these, older people won't protect themselves by selling off their stock and keeping more money in cash. Then when the market goes down, you get a panic reaction.

Consider a couple that put $200,000 into stocks twenty years ago and now finds the stock worth $1 million. Because of high capital gains tax, they refuse to sell. Even if a falling market reduces the value of their portfolio to $900,000, they still won't sell. Finally, when their portfolio is only worth $600,000 or $700,000, they may very well panic and sell for fear of losing everything they worked for their whole lives.

That's a tragedy. Older people are much more inclined to sell at lower prices than they are at higher prices for fear that their hard-earned money will get totally wiped out. The result of their not selling is a stepped-up basis on death. It is a mis-allocation of resources on a national basis. People over seventy years of age should be slowly pulling their money out of stocks. Instead, they are forced by high capital gains taxes into a zero or 100 percent game determined by an event—death—that presumably they don't have any control over. Who knows whether you are going to die at a market peak or a market trough?

The villain in the piece is not the old person who resents having to pay such high taxes. It's the tax itself. In California, the combined state and federal capital gains tax is about 35 percent. Let me tell you, that is one tough bogie. The fastest way to turn $1 million into $600,000 is to liquidate all the securities while you are still alive.

You don't have to play this 100 percent or nothing game. There's a better way. Sell something every year. If you decide at age seventy that 80 percent of your portfolio in stocks is too much, then sell 5 percent of your stock that year. You don't have to sell all the stock and you don't have to say, "I'm not going to pay the government anything." You pay taxes on 5 percent of your stocks. Yes, it's painful, but it is better than not doing anything to protect yourself from risk.

The second year, sell another 5 percent of your stock. Do the same thing the third year. Hopefully the market is still going up, and—this is a concept no one buys at all—the bull market pays your taxes. In 1995, the market went up 37 percent. You could have sold all your stock and the market would have paid all your taxes.

Of course, most people don't see it that way. They see taxation and their wealth as two totally separate matters. They deserve their 37 percent increase. The government doesn't deserve its taxes. If you had $3 million at the beginning of 1995 and you had $4 million at the end of the year, that $4 million is yours—you earned it fair and square, and you'll be damned if you are going to give any of it to the government if you can avoid it.

Can you sell some part of $4 million?

Sure.

Will you have to pay a huge tax?

Yes.

What do you do?

Sell 5 percent, which is $200,000. You pay $70,000 in taxes. That still leaves you with $130,000 to stick in a bank, a checking account, a savings account, or a money market fund. Put it in ninety-day T-bills, five-year notes, or ten-year bonds.

Under the Capital Market Pricing Model, if you take less risk, you can expect lower returns, but that's okay when you're seventy years old. What you're trying to do at that age is maximize your risk-adjusted rate of return.

Achieving the maximum inflation-adjusted, after-tax, risk-adjusted rate of return is what we are all trying to do.

A Formula for Balancing Stocks Versus Age

As you get older, you generally want to decrease your reliance on stocks and increase your reliance on bonds and cash equivalents. There is probably no age at which you should get out of stocks entirely, but the kinds of stocks you own will change over time.

Let's assume there are no tax consequences and no capital gains taxes, and everyone either has 401ks or IRA rollovers. There used to be an old rule of thumb that said the percentage of your assets invested in stocks should be one hundred minus your age. So if you were fifty years old, you would have 50 percent of your portfolio in stocks. If you were sixty years old, you would have 40 percent in stocks. If you were ninety years old, you would have 10 percent in stocks.

That may have been reasonable for people fifty years ago. However, people are living so much longer now that the formula doesn't apply today. And in any case you want to take as much risk as possible when you're younger. I don't know what the new starting number is; maybe it's 115. Maybe the calculation should start from the last age at which it is still reasonable to be 100 percent in stocks and calculate from there. If it is reasonable to be 100 percent in stocks at age thirty, then use 130, and subtract your age from that.

The number may differ by person and attitude. If you are never comfortable being 100 percent in stocks, then fine. If you think you should be only 80 percent in stocks at age thirty, then use 110 as your starting number. If you want to be just 50 percent in stocks at age thirty, then use 80 as your starting number.

No matter what number you start with when subtracting your age, you still should never have less than 10 percent to 20 percent of your portfolio in stocks. According to the actuarial tables, a person who is ninety-five years of age can expect on average to live another three years. The last thing you want to do is run out of money in your old age.

Assuming you are always going to keep 10 to 20 percent of your assets in stock no matter how old you are, you will probably want a combination of low volatility stocks and growth stocks. You might very well live to be 110. Sixty to seventy percent of all medical spending takes place in the last six months of your life.

When are the last six months of your life?

That's why you always want to keep some assets in stock— you won't know that until after the fact.

The Case for Work

When planning for retirement, there are a couple of things you should always keep in mind: the purchasing power advantage of rolling money-market funds or ninety-day T-bills is zero; stocks give you a higher return over time because you take more risk. If you are ninety years old and have a $50 million portfolio, you've reached orbital velocity. You can take all the risk you want at any age. If you live another twenty years and they take away 80 percent of your money, you've still got a lot of money.

The big question is how long do you expect to have to live on your money? If it's a long time, then even a big pile of money might not look like much. You also want to take into consideration the life expectancy of the surviving spouse— that changes how much money is a lot of money real fast.

Remember the fellow with cancer whose wife was expected to outlive him by thirty-five to forty-five years? The first time we ran the numbers for them, she ran out of money in twenty-seven years, but eventually we found an arrangement that would ensure her financial security for her whole life. We were able to do that in his case, because he had $2 million in assets to play with. But suppose he didn't. What could he do?

Well, lots of things: his wife could work, he could leave less money to the children, or, since his cancer was in remission, he might delay retirement as long as possible. If he could work another five years, all his wife's potential money problems would be solved without any need to make concessions. It would be five years in which he was not taking money out of his portfolio but building it up.

Working past your normal retirement age really makes a huge difference. Every year that you are able to add to your assets rather than subtract from them is just gargantuan in its impact. My recommendation to someone who is fifty-five years old, in poor health, and worried about his wife's welfare is: Make sure you don't die. Don't die last year for sure. Don't die next year. And work. Don't take money out. Get a job.

—⁓⁓—

CHAPTER 11

———◦◦◦———

Researching Problems

Before you buy a stock, you always want to look at: 1) its market-capitalization-to-revenues, 2) its Relative Dividend Yield, and 3) its price-to-book value. You also want an idea of whether the stock is at the high, middle, or low end of its range.

If the stock is expensive, you don't want to own it. If it is fair valued or cheap, you may want to buy it. You should never get caught in a situation where you have to make short-term predictions. Because of the noise factor, it's impossible to know what a stock will do next week, next month, or next quarter. You want to look far enough out that you can deal with averages. Assume every stock will go to fair value in five years. Clearly, you want to start with cheap stocks, if for no other reason than cheap stocks tend to go up and expensive stocks tend to go down.

Don't extrapolate to infinity or to oblivion. The faster the growth, the higher the price you can pay, but it's hard to sustain above-average growth rates. By the same token, below-average growth rates are hard to sustain too. Either the company crashes or the sustained period of underperformance demonstrates that the current management can't handle the problem. So you look outside for new leadership. At worst, the company gets acquired by people who know what they are doing.

No investor should ever be a friend of management, because being a friend of management assumes that current people are the solution. That's impossible to know. Maybe they are, and maybe they aren't. When you own cheap stocks, though, you don't care as much whether today's management is the solution or not. You only have to be convinced that over, say, the next five years someone is going to fix whatever is broken.

What Business Are You In?

When you encounter a company whose stock is very cheap, the first thing you want to know as an investor is whether it has had a structural breakdown that will take more than five years to fix or if it has a problem that is readily fixable. Is the company a bicycle with a bent and broken frame, or does the company just have a flat tire?

The company isn't working in either situation, but in one case the company just has a minor problem while in the other case the company's problems are structural: perhaps the industry has undergone a fundamental shift and has left this company standing in the dust, or perhaps the company doesn't understand its true function within the industry.

As a famous article in the *Harvard Business Review* once pointed out, you have to know what business you are in. If railroads had thought of themselves not as railroads but as transportation companies, they might have found it a lot easier to deal with the competition from trucking companies. IBM thought it was in the mainframe business instead of in a bigger, broader business called information technology, and it went through some very hard years as a result.

Digital Equipment Corporation (DEC) thought it was in the minicomputer business, and it consequently lost a commanding lead. If only the people at DEC had taken this attitude: "Boy, these cheap PCs make terrific terminals. All we have to do is take a bunch of PCs and attach them to our minicomputer with a local area network." It might have ended up a totally different company. Instead, DEC tried to compete *with* desktop PCs, while all these other companies came in and started making servers. DEC blew a golden opportunity. The desktops have moved up to become servers, and DEC was already there. The industry was undergoing a structural change, but DEC didn't see it coming.

Structural change in technology takes place very slowly at first; then suddenly everything changes overnight. When Dr. Wang invented core magnetic memory, everyone thought it would be here forever; then the world moved to hard drives. Nowadays everyone assumes that hard drives are going to disappear the same way. But—another surprise—so far they've been a moving target technology, getting both faster and larger in capacity while their price is still going down.

The same is true of television. Anything analog is going to be defunct in the next ten years. People who understand that they are not in the television business but are in the information image business will be the ones who come out on top.

Remember Zenith? It couldn't adapt to a structural change. It advertised its sets as "hand-wired," but nobody cared. Nobody wanted less reliability and higher cost when they could get cheaper sets with printed circuit boards from overseas. The consumer was better served by *not* having hand-wired TV sets.

VCRs are a Russian invention that we appropriated. All the original VCRs were made here. Quasar was an American company once owned by Motorola; now it's gone, sold. All the VCR action now is overseas.

When you see a technology company in trouble, you have to ask these questions: Is the company up against a structural shift with which there's no way to cope? Or is management doing things that perhaps are not showing up yet but nevertheless really do make a lot of sense?

A Company That Understands Its Business

By 1990, Merrill Lynch, a former great growth stock, was a broken and battered one. Whereas in 1983 the stock had been over 26, by October of 1990 it was down to barely 9. Relative Dividend Yield (RDY) calculations told us it was cheap. But before we bought the stock, we needed to know one thing: Was Merrill Lynch suffering from inherent structural problems, or did it have a problem that good management could fix?

We visited the company a couple of times. We talked to analysts. Then we watched the management do two things that showed it was focused on the problem: it directly attacked costs by leasing out a couple of floors in its NYC financial center, and it started spreading out the commission payments to the brokers.

The fact that brokers moved around so much had always been a major problem for companies like Merrill Lynch. Spreading out their commission payments would make it harder for brokers to take their last month's check, walk across the street, and go to work for the competition.

When we looked at Merrill Lynch, we liked what we saw. Its stock was cheap on an RDY basis, and the company was taking steps to restore profitability. We didn't know everything there was to know about Merrill Lynch, and we certainly could have taken a financial bath. As an outsider, there's no way to know everything about a given company. That's why you want a diversified portfolio. If you own twenty stocks, your portfolio isn't just the sum of twenty independent analytical decisions; there has to be some interrelationship of the pieces. If we knew how to own just one stock, we would. It would make life so much simpler. But it's too dangerous to own just one stock, so we protect ourselves with diversification, especially by buying the stocks of companies that are solidly focused and understanding what business they are really in.

The Quality, Consistency, Clean Restrooms Business

Years ago, a neighbor of mine invested all his money in McDonald's. One day, McDonald's switched from bleached pulp white paper bags to brown paper bags, and my neighbor threw a fit. "That's it!" he said. "They blew it. McDonald's has caved in to the ecologists."

Of course it was pure nonsense to think that just because McDonald's was switching to brown paper bags and cardboard containers it was being taken over by radical environmental loonies who would end up killing the company. On the contrary, McDonald's had just figured out what was essential to its business and what was not. It knew what business it was really in.

McDonald's didn't start out that way. Back in the mid-sixties, its stores weren't open at breakfast—they only served lunch and dinner. Every store had to prepare its French fries from fresh potatoes on the premises. Hamburger was ground by local butchers. The company had a policy of not hiring women.

Those points were originally viewed as absolutely essential to McDonald's success, but somewhere along the line, company management began to rethink all its old assumptions: "We are making French fries from raw potatoes in every store, but Simplot is offering to sell us frozen French fries by the truckload and the customers don't know the difference. So let's do frozen French fries."

Then management had another thought: "Boy, we are really being taken advantage of by the local meat providers, because there is a season for cattle but our demand isn't seasonal and they know we need to buy fresh ground meat. Why don't we buy frozen patties? Our customers don't care."

Finally the company reconsidered its policy on workers: "We're running out of men to hire, particularly at noon. Women are available. We could get them to work two or three hours in the middle of the day while their kids are in school."

So McDonald's started hiring women, ditched the fresh ground beef, and began cooking frozen French fries. The company just sorted it out and decided that what people really wanted was quality and consistency, one location to another, and clean bathrooms.

It used to be that all McDonald's stores looked the same: big yellow double arches and red-and-white tile in the stores. This look continued until people started to complain. Now, for example, in Freeport, Maine, there's a McDonald's in an old house. One wouldn't even know it was a McDonald's except for one small sign.

Some people might say that McDonald's was greedy because it would do anything, including abandon its own standards, to make more money. Not true. It was merely forced to understand the true essence of its business. McDonald's is in the business of providing quality, consistency, and convenience of location, and the company determined that it was far easier to achieve its real goals by using frozen French fries and meat and by hiring women. The ideas that management used to hold near and dear were actually false to successful business.

It's the Sauce

There used to be a company called Lums, which is now bankrupt. In the sixties, I was at a computer conference in Anaheim, California, where I overheard a group of growth stock managers trading stories; eventually the conversation got around to Lums. This was back in the ego-driven, late-sixties environment, in which everyone had a hot stock or hot idea. One man at the conference was really hot on Lums. When asked why, he said, "It's the sauce!"

When I heard that, I nearly choked. It reminded me of the time during the height of the real estate mania when a man literally grabbed me by the lapels and said, "It's the dirt!"

If you're going to invest in stock, you have to learn to avoid getting swept up in the fads of the day. You have to make sure a company has some long-term advantages that can't be easily replicated. You have to take a look at the capital constraints to competition. That's one reason why companies have such a tough time going head to head with McDonald's—its overall spending on advertising is very large, but its spending on advertising per unit of sales is very small.

That's pretty tough to compete with.

Large-Scale Mistakes

Years ago, Schlitz was a pretender to the number one spot in beer sales. People had written reports claiming that Schlitz was about to knock Budweiser off the top position. But Budweiser's advertising budget, which was three times as big as Schlitz's, cost Bud one-fourth as much per barrel.

In such a case, you would have to figure that if Schlitz really was better than Bud, how much better was it? What kind of growth would it need to have in market share increases, and how would the company achieve it? If Schlitz, for instance, spent $6 a barrel for advertising and Bud spent only $1.50, it couldn't have a price war with Bud to gain market share, because Bud would have a $4.50 advantage for every barrel sold. So Schlitz had to gain market share on service, on having a better product, or on buyer perception. Otherwise, Budweiser would clean it out.

Up to this time, Schlitz had been looking pretty good, but then it made a major mistake: it changed its beer recipe by shortening the brewing time. Now, I'm not a beer aficionado; I don't know if this changed the taste or not. But once beer drinkers heard that Schlitz was brewed less, they assumed it was an inferior product. At this point, Schlitz was basically dead, whereas at one point it had been a real, live competitor.

When you're looking for good investments, you will find some companies that can be restored to financial health quickly and you will find other companies with basic structural problems that no amount of good management can ever overcome. As an investor, you want to find companies that other investors see as having insurmountable problems but that you recognize as basically sound companies with a few temporary woes.

Management Mistakes

When I first started following U.S. Surgical, it was a tiny company in Norwalk, Connecticut. It was started by a salesman without a college degree, Leon Hirsch, and a Hungarian immigrant who handled the technology. They began with 85 percent of market share in the procedure called skin stapling. Later, they got into general surgical instrumentation and were pioneers in laparoscopic surgery.

In laparoscopic surgery, instead of opening up a patient's entire abdomen for an operation, four small incisions are made. It's much less invasive than conventional surgery. The patient heals faster and gets out of the hospital sooner. U.S. Surgical basically invented this procedure. At the start, it had 90 percent market share, then it dropped to 85 percent market share; pretty soon it was losing market share all over the place. Its primary competition was Johnson & Johnson. If one has to have a competitor, Johnson & Johnson is a good company to be in competition with, as it has a real profit motivation and doesn't cut prices to drive people out of business.

Even though U.S. Surgical lost its monopoly, dropping from 90 percent market share down to 55, it was still doing fine. Fifty-five percent wasn't a monopoly, but it wasn't bad, and it was a lot better than having none of the market at all.

Hirsch, unfortunately, couldn't accept that. Hirsch is a very tenacious, aggressive guy. That is both the good news and the bad news. He went on a rampage against Johnson & Johnson, making speeches against them and attacking them in public.

Johnson & Johnson is a huge, successful, and well-run company. In a head-to-head battle, there's no way U.S. Surgical is going to come out on top. Pretty soon, its stock had fallen from 140 to 16.

At that point, Hirsch reassessed the situation. He had worked too hard to help build U.S. Surgical, and he wasn't willing to lose it as a result of his own or anyone else's ego. He backed off from challenging Johnson & Johnson and went to work on his own company's expenses and products. U.S. Surgical eventually came back, and the stock rose to 43.

That's the story of U.S. Surgical. Let me tell you what happened to us. Because U.S. Surgical was such a highly volatile company, many investors got trapped by taxes into keeping its stock longer than they should have. My firm bought stock when it was about 20, and by the time it hit 80 or 85, it was overvalued. That was the time to take our profits and get out. We did sell some stock in some accounts, but then it went to 140, and we looked like fools—for a short time anyway.

Even so, when we looked at the company's market-cap-to-revenues, it was clear that 140 was not a real number. U.S. Surgical had about 60 million shares out and revenues of $1.2 billion. This gave them a market cap of over $8 billion when the stock was 140, and a market-cap-to-revenues of about seven times. Even being wildly optimistic that its revenues would grow 50 percent in one year, to $1.8 billion, the stock was still absurdly expensive. It made sense for our clients to sell at 140 and pay the taxes on the investment.

No one wants to pay that much in taxes. It's like sitting there and watching the stock drop overnight from 85 to 50.

It's a hard call to make. What if you don't do it, and U.S. Surgical drops 90 percent to 15 or 16?

There are times when it pays to pay the taxes.

When the Economics Just Aren't There

As a kid, I used to read *Popular Science* magazine. I remember stories predicting that everyone would soon have helicopters in their garage and no one would ever worry about traffic jams anymore. Well, the years have passed, and nothing remotely like that has ever happened.

It's a matter of economics. Things won't happen if the numbers don't add up. Sometimes you find a well-managed company with a first-class product and it's a leader in its field, but the economics just aren't there.

Years ago, I followed a chemical company in Palo Alto that had good people, great labs, and terrific technology. It came up with a new chemical that was terrific for killing mosquito larvae; it was ecologically sound, and technically elegant. Unfortunately, it was also inordinately expensive compared to the old method, which was to buy a barrel of used-engine oil for fifty cents and pour it over the swamp. It killed the mosquitoes just as dead and was a heck of a lot cheaper. Would you want to spend fifty cents for old engine oil or $100 for an elegant biotech solution?

Old engine oil is not pretty, and ecologically it is not the most sound. Yet when something costs two hundred times as much as some other solution, it really has to be great, especially in a place like Africa, where few people have $100 anyway.

Success in these matters often comes down to simple economics.

Investing in Technology

When you're an investor, you're always looking for a company that will make a technological breakthrough and come up with a real structural change. The automobile was a real structural change. So were telephones, airplanes, and transistors. What will be next?

I'm betting on the full-frame, color, video telephone transmitted through a personal computer. It isn't just a telephone with pictures. It's going to change the whole world.

Should you therefore pay any price for the companies involved? I don't think so. For one thing, nobody knows yet what companies will provide that structurally different service. As an example, if you were to go back forty years to the time the transistor was invented and ask which companies would turn out to be the transistor companies, people would probably pick the vacuum tube companies, such as RCA. They had the distribution. They had the capability. They were already in the business of making parts for radios and TVs. But RCA is not in the transistor business today, and the average person on the street wouldn't even know who RCA is.

Similarly, no one knows who will be the winners in the video telephone business. If I had to take a guess, I'd say the telephone companies are going to be the suppliers and conduits. I don't think you are going to see any independent cable companies offering video telephone service. There never was any economic justification for cable companies in the first place, and except for a federal judge there wouldn't even have been a cable industry. The cable companies are going to become part of the telephone company, which is what they should have been in the first place.

The economics all argue for the telephone companies. All that's needed are two coaxial cables and four twisted pairs, wound together in a factory. All the expenses come from putting them on poles or trenches through existing rights-of-way. Hooking up the customers is cheap; cable can be installed with a screwdriver. It might cost the company perhaps $10 to hook up a customer; then the company can turn around and charge the customer $20 a month from there on out. That's good business.

Two-way interactive video telephone is not that far away—a year or two at most. When it arrives, it will be a major structural change. Instead of connecting a one-way cable to your TV, you'll connect a two-way cable to your television or computer. This is why I think one-way satellite television dishes are temporary and two-way cable is not. You can't have two-way communications with a little pizza-pan satellite dish on your roof. For two-way, you need land-line cables. Once those are up and running, a telephone company may offer for $20 a month what you now pay $30 a month for from a cable company. It's going to drive cable companies out of business.

It is very hard to figure where cable companies have a competitive advantage over the telephone companies. They don't offer cheaper costs, better service, or more service people. One could argue that the coaxial cable is already in place, while the phone companies have only two-way twisted pairs of copper wire. Still, if the model is two-way interactive, then telephone companies are already there; they don't have to switch their thinking. My guess is that a separate cable industry won't even exist five years from now.

This doesn't mean that cable companies are not good investments. It depends on their attitude. If they try to compete with the phone company, then stay away, because they will surely go the way of buggy-whip companies. If, on the other hand, the cable companies understand that they are there to be broken up—"Here I am. Here are all my miles of cables and thousands of subscribers. Take me apart."—they will be acquired by big wealthy telephone companies and make their shareholders rich.

Clarity, Consistency, and Boredom

Even though our clients love it when we make money for them, they are still disappointed that so much of what we buy is, frankly, boring. We don't buy glamour stocks. We don't buy high-tech. Sometimes when I hear this I ask them, "Do you want to be excited or do you want to be wealthy?"

Still, I understand their complaints. You do end up with boring companies when buying with the RDY method. Not only that, when we buy a cheap stock by price-to-book, market cap, or RDY, sooner or later a client will tell us that buying that stock was a crummy idea. Each of our clients owns forty to sixty stocks, and eventually every stock gets attacked.

Sometimes the critics are right. Stocks don't get cheap without a problem, and big-company stocks don't get cheap without everybody knowing about the problem. The issue always comes down to whether or not the problem is factored into the price of the stock. We don't care about the ten best reasons not to own a stock. What we want to know is whether or not the stock is cheap because the *market* already knows those ten reasons.

By the same token, we also don't care about the ten best reasons never to sell a stock. If the stock is expensive because ten positive reasons are already reflected in the price, then we sell, which is fine. We're not journalists. We're not trying to figure out the ten worst things about JC Penney at 40 or the ten best things about Netscape today.

Our goal is to figure out which stocks will make our clients money. Some of these Internet companies come on the market, and everyone goes crazy; I have trouble figuring out what is unique about them. How much of what we see is just puff and fluff and smoke and mirrors? No one has a clue. For example, how many employees are at Yahoo!? Where did it get its program? Is there any sustainability? What are the structural problems?

Netscape may or may not be the next Microsoft. Intuit may or may not be the next Microsoft. It's very unlikely they both will become the next Microsoft. The question to ask today is whether Microsoft is the next Microsoft.

Polaroid was supposed to be the next Xerox, except there was no next Xerox—even Xerox wasn't the next Xerox. Burroughs was supposed to be the next IBM. When DEC was the number two computer company, it made a big deal of the fact. I thought, "Wait a minute. What's so great about being number two when number one isn't even number one anymore? Are the conditions really there for IBM to be IBM again?"

Our company has a long and, some would say, somewhat checkered history with IBM. Back in the early 1980s, at the Bank of California, we sold IBM when it was at $124. At that point, it was the eighth largest trade ever done on the New York Stock Exchange. We represented a woman who had a huge block of IBM stock. She died in a new tax year, which meant her estate could sell without any tax consequence.

For us, the question was whether IBM at 124 was cheap, expensive, or fair valued. If it was cheap, we'd hold on to the stock. If it was expensive, we'd sell. We decided it was expensive, and we sold the whole block. Eventually it went up to 150, and then it dropped sharply.

A decade later, we started buying IBM again when the price dropped below 100 and it started to look cheap to us. Even though the management had cut the dividend from $4.86 to $2.12, the price by this time was down to 50, and to us it looked very attractive. Then, in 1993, former Nabisco CEO Louis Gerstner took over, and for various reasons (not the least of which was ego and wanting to start over with a clean house) he proceeded to throw everything out but the kitchen sink. He cut the dividend to $1, which brought IBM's yield way below the market.

We had bought IBM in the mid- to high-seventies. But because of the dividend cut, it was now expensive, so in line with our RDY strategy we sold it in the mid- to high-forties. Misjudging Gerstner was our big mistake for the year. We didn't think he had to cut the dividends. I still don't. The company was wading in cash.

On the other hand, it didn't make any difference to our strategy why the dividend had been cut. Once it had been cut, we had to sell. A cheap-stock strategy won't work if you don't apply it consistently. A portfolio that contains one stock that is owned on a different theory than all the other stocks is really two portfolios—a multistock portfolio and a portfolio of just one stock. When we talk about the need for diversification in one's portfolio, that's not the kind we mean.

Still More Thoughts on Diversification

First principles: If a portfolio isn't more than just the sum of the parts, you aren't doing it right. In a truly diversified portfolio, the individual stocks don't react to external events in the same way, with all the issues simultaneously moving up or down. You want economic diversification. You want to make sure, if you've got ten stocks, that they have some global aspects to them. You don't want ten companies that all feed the auto industry. They may be different kinds of companies—glass, tires, windshields—but if the end-buyer is the same person, that's not diversification. Why even bother?

This problem plagued the old Nifty Fifty stocks in 1972. People took big hits financially, because on the surface the Nifty Fifty looked like a diversified portfolio, but all the stocks were owned for the same reasons: great balance sheets, high margins, and stability of earnings growth. There was no diversification of stock characteristics, though the companies were spread out in fifteen or twenty industries. McDonald's was the same as Procter & Gamble, and Procter & Gamble was the same as Eastman Kodak. That was why investors bought them.

Another problem with the Nifty Fifty lay in the fact that they were promulgated by a relatively few banks—J. P. Morgan in particular—all of whom thought they had discovered the secrets to the universe.

It's always easy to discover the secrets of the universe looking backward. Anyone can tell you what the winners *were,* and then make up some rational explanation why they won. The test is not in proving what *happened* but in predicting what *will happen.*

Some people try to protect themselves against risk by padding their portfolio with just one industry, such as electrical utilities. If you own only ten stocks, however, you probably don't want to own more than one electrical utility. If you own twenty stocks, you may want to own two. Forty stocks, you may want to own five. Sixty stocks, you may want to own ten, which is more or less the number that we own.

The problem is that most individual investors don't want to mess around with that many, so they buy their local utility and let it go at that, which is terrible. They may be in an awful regulatory commission area; the utility might be 100 percent on the wrong fuel; the utility may service a highly cyclical business in which people lose their jobs and the utility loses its primary business. In a case like that, you don't reduce your risk with one or two electrical utilities—you only make it worse.

Don't Follow the Crowd

Although many investors regard technology stocks as exciting, new and hot technology doesn't always pan out. Typically, someone comes up with a breakthrough. There's a big article about it in *Fortune* magazine. Then you don't hear of it again for ten years, at which time it pops out and finally goes somewhere.

Technology is nice and technology is clearly a driver, but ultimately, it is management and the ability to control the technology that lead to super-winner companies and super-winner stocks. Companies like Hewlett-Packard and Motorola have been terrific long-term successes, but not simply because of technology alone. They also know how to manage the technology, and that is a very different thing.

Three years ago, Motorola was so cheap its market-cap-to-revenues were less than one. Then the stock took off—it literally soared. By the fall of 1996, it had cooled again.

This is why I say the stock market is over half psychology. When Motorola or Intel are cheap again, the thinking is going to be, "They were once great technological companies, but they will never have earnings growth again. The industry has matured, and now they are just commodity businesses." Some of this psychology results from the media's perpetual stories on the ten best reasons to own or not own a stock. At peaks and bottoms, you'll always get those ten reasons. But if you are going to make money buying cheap stocks, you really have to think differently from the rest of the herd. You can't be a sheep, you can't be a penguin. You have to be different. You can't get sucked in.

If someone says, "It's guaranteed. It's a no-brainer. I bought it for my grandmother," be careful. But if someone says, "I wouldn't touch that with a ten-foot pole," maybe it's something you ought to investigate. You may discover that the company is going down the drain, management doesn't know what it's doing, and the company is filing for bankruptcy next week. But you should at least come to these unloved stocks with a positive bias: "I want to own this stock unless I find out bad things."

With expensive stocks, do just the opposite. Approach them with a negative bias: "I shouldn't own that company unless it's really terrific." Or, "I should sell that company unless someone can convince me otherwise."

One thing I've discovered is that most of the time people can't come up with even one good reason, let alone ten, to buy expensive stocks. They will give you reasons, but the reasons don't make sense. Often, the argument simply comes down to "Because it's going up."

Many people find that a compelling argument. People who buy Microsoft regardless of the price will argue that value is meaningless—book value doesn't mean anything, yield doesn't mean anything, market-cap-to-revenues doesn't mean anything. In some cases, they might be right. If you look at the relationship of price to these other values, there is no absolute number. On the other hand, there is a historical relationship, and if you look at that you will see that Microsoft's price-to-book is very high. If you look at market-cap-to-revenues, you will see it is quite expensive, and this is taking into account the fact that an $8 billion company will generally have a lower market cap compared to revenue than it did when it had only $100 million in revenues.

When you dismiss all those reasons, people will still want to go out and buy Microsoft: "It has been a terrific company. Bill Gates is a terrific guy." That's true, but it's also past tense. It's water under the bridge. And besides, all those points are already reflected in the price of the stock. It still doesn't matter to most people. They will rationalize paying over 100 for the stock by saying, "Its future earnings are going to grow faster than its PE." Yes, but the numbers that people use to determine whether a stock is cheap or not move over time. In 1972 or 1973, stocks were thought to be cheap at two to three times their growth rates; now it's one.

It's all rationalization. People will say everyone who was worried about the price ten, eight, six, four, or two years ago was wrong. That's true, looking back. But you're not looking back, you're looking forward. And when you look forward, you find that you want the answer to another question entirely: Is Microsoft going to be the one stock in ten thousand where value doesn't count? Consider the odds. In poker, you can get four kings, but the odds against that are so high that you wouldn't want to bet the farm.

With institutions, on the other hand, it's a lot easier to bet the farm. That is one big difference between institutions and individuals. Individuals typically understand odds better—it is their money and their farms, and they aren't going to risk them on whims. The typical institutional investor is more than willing to bet someone else's farm—simply for ego if nothing else.

This isn't to say that everyone has the discipline, approach, or thought process to be a good investor. Clearly it's very hard to be a contrarian investor. Going with the crowd is easy. It's a way to hide.

If it is a bull market, that's terrific. Will it always be a bull market? I'd like to think so, but reality tells me otherwise.

The Crowd Isn't Always Wrong

Most investors are growth stock buyers. They don't care whether stocks are expensive or cheap. The important thing to them is that the stock is going up.

We, in contrast, are contrarians. If we own a stock that goes up so much it gets overvalued, we sell it. We don't try to buy at the absolute bottom, and we don't try to sell at the absolute top. That's too hard. We would much rather be sure not to buy at the top or sell at the bottom, which is a much easier thing to do.

When I describe myself as contrarian, I don't mean a whirling dervish contrarian, the kind who just looks at what the crowd is doing and does the opposite. That's foolish. For one thing, the crowd is not *always* wrong. When the crowd is in the middle, which is to say neither foolishly positive over a stock nor terminally negative, I might well conclude that being with the crowd is fine. If they haven't pushed a stock up so much that it is expensive, I might very well want to climb on their shoulders for a while and go along for the ride. The crowd isn't usually right for long, but it is silly to claim, as some contrarians do, that the crowd is always wrong by definition.

Now, you don't want to follow the crowd everywhere. At stock bottoms, you want to be contrary. Peaks occur when everyone else wants to buy. Bottoms occur when everyone else wants to sell. If everyone is buying, thus driving a stock

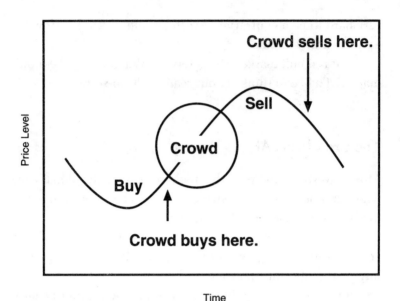

Figure 11.1   *Where the Crowd Buys and Sells*

up, that's when we get off. If everyone is selling, driving a stock down, that's when we buy (see Figure 11.1).

Here's an example: Merck is one of those stocks that, through June of 1991, had not sold above 80 percent of the market yield. People loved the stock when it was 55 and the yield was low in relation to the market. It was expensive to us, though, because we are not interested in any stock that is not at least at a 25 percent premium above the S&P 500 (RDY = 1.25).

As Merck stock got cheaper and cheaper, however, the crowd reversed itself and by 30 had totally abandoned the stock. To us, that was the point at which Merck looked really good. It was selling at a 30 to 35 percent premium over the market yield, and no one else was interested in it. For six months, it could be bought at 29, 30, 33, 31, 30, or 29.

Eventually, however, it started to rise again. At this point, the crowd caught on that Merck was not going into the abyss. Everyone jumped back in at 35 to 40. For us, it was more expensive than before, but still not so expensive that we wanted to sell. So we and the crowd both agreed that Merck was good to own.

It didn't stay that way for long. The crowd kept pushing and pushing, and at some point in the low 40s, we said good-bye. Eventually, the crowd pushed the stock up to 70, but by that time we were long gone.

Cheap Versus Value

Institutional investors make a distinction between value stocks and growth stocks, but it's the wrong distinction. If you ask these investors if they buy regardless of value, they say no. One of my cofounders, Ken Kaplan, gives a speech in which he argues that there is no such thing as a valueless investor. It's true. They may use a hokey, meaningless measure of value. They may look at value in terms of growth rate versus PE. But nobody buys a stock saying, "I know it's overvalued, but I'm going to buy it anyway."

Individual investors, on the other hand, place stocks in three broad categories: cheap, expensive, and fair valued, which is the right way to do it. This is another case where the individual investor is a lot better off than the institutional investor, who in my opinion doesn't know value from cheap from growth.

This was one of the things that sandbagged me on Polaroid. None of the senior people stepped back and said, "Yes, it's a growth stock, but the growth is already in the price of the stock. No matter how fast it grows it's still expensive."

I would guess that 90 percent of the analysts on Wall Street are oriented toward growth stocks. They simply don't pay attention to value (what we call cheapness). To an institution, a value stock is one that hasn't done well and thus can be bought at a bargain price. On this point we and the institutional investors agree. The difference is that most institutions don't on that account go out and buy the stock, which they really would if they believed it was such a good value. Instead, they buy a stock that has appreciated and call it a growth stock.

There's a big difference between appreciation and growth. Sometimes earnings can grow really rapidly, but the stock is so expensive to begin with that its price really doesn't rise. Xerox, for example, was a growth stock, but it hit its peak price way before the company's earnings growth rate ever slowed. The stock stopped doing well five or eight years before the company started to have competitive problems.

New Rules, New Game

"Always" is not a great word to use in the markets, because just as soon as everyone understands the rules, the game changes. What worked in the market yesterday suddenly doesn't work today. Everyone used to pay huge attention to the weekly money supply numbers, which were reported every Friday afternoon. New Yorkers didn't like that, because they wanted to take off early on Fridays, so the reports started coming out on Thursdays. Soon, weekly money supply numbers were ignored. No one even pays attention to them anymore.

Another rule was a common agreement that cyclical stocks were cyclical forever. Then the game changed, and cyclicals suddenly turned into growth/cyclicals or even occasionally flipped back to being growth stocks.

Cyclicals, Growth Stocks, and Growth/Cyclicals

Cyclicals are stocks that alternate between being growth and value, between being expensive and being cheap. With a little higher price, they become growth/cyclicals. Some of these make it to a steady growth stock status. At bull market peaks, however, real growth stocks don't just slowly become cyclicals again. Something happens, and there is an abyss.

IBM at 45 or 50 was a cyclical. IBM at 80 or 90 was a growth/cyclical. At 120, it was a growth stock again. Coca Cola, in 1982, was a cyclical. By 1985, it was a growth/cyclical. Since 1987–88, it has been a growth stock.

Whether a stock is a cyclical, a growth/cyclical, or a growth stock is more about investor attitude than anything else. It's much more subjective than investors think of it at the time.

Pick up any financial magazine, and you can get lists of stocks that supposedly will grow consistently during the next ten years. You could have found similar lists in 1972. They weren't right in those days, either. In 1972, Avon was at 120; Polaroid was over 140. The lists focused on the Tier One growth stocks and the Nifty Fifty. Out of 1972's Nifty Fifty, only ten or twelve would be on a Nifty Fifty today—among them Procter & Gamble, Caterpillar, and Eastman Kodak.

During the 1973–74 bear market, these former growth stocks became cyclicals. People said, "Oh sure, their earnings are going to go up a lot, but it won't last." The earnings did go up, and the same people said, "Well, yes, they have above-average earnings growth, but it is highly volatile."

It's all attitude. With the passage of time, investors often see the same stock in a different light. Between 1973–74 and today, there is no company among the Nifty Fifty that wasn't described at some time as a cyclical or growth/cyclical. Some have never gotten above being growth/cyclicals, and some have languished as cyclicals. Coca-Cola came back to growth status. Procter & Gamble did the same. Dow Chemical got as high as growth/cyclical, then fell back to cyclical.

The issue is never whether a stock is a growth stock or not; the issue is the price. We never buy stocks regardless of price. I'm not adverse to buying low-yield stocks. What I am adverse to is buying stocks regardless of the price. What we do for private clients is low-yield investing. We bifurcate our clients' portfolios. We don't find any comfort in the middle. When you start out with average yield, average growth, and average characteristics, you end up with average results.

What you want to do is look at the ends where the people mostly aren't. Look at companies that are out of favor. It doesn't matter if they are high or low yield. Those come at both ends. Whether it is U.S. Surgical at 35 or Exxon at 81, Baltimore Gas and Electric or Wisconsin Energy, it doesn't matter as long as they are hated, unloved, out of favor, and thus inexpensive. Sometimes you find companies that are both high yield and expensive. Those are dangerous, and we try to stay away from them.

We are much more interested in Teradyne at 15 than at 60. Teradyne is not a yield stock. It's a technology stock. It's a growth/cyclical stock—at its peak it's a growth stock; at its bottom it's a cyclical stock. The attitude of investors toward the stock is far more volatile than the company's prospects really warrant.

CHAPTER 12

The Opening Door of
Your Future

When I was in college, plastic dry-cleaning bags had just been introduced; someone used one to cover a pillow, and it suffocated a child. Subsequently, a huge movement arose to outlaw plastic dry-cleaning bags.

The movement was supported by the paper dry-cleaning bag companies, which should come as no surprise. Does that mean that paper dry-cleaning bag companies are evil? No. It means that any time there is a shift or change, someone invariably sees it as a crisis. Predicting imminent economic or environmental disaster seems to satisfy a perverse need in some people. Maybe they like the drama of feeling they are living in the last days, when every word or deed matters. In the 1980s, a famous TV actor said he didn't want to be alive in ten years, given how fast the environment seemed to be falling apart. During the 1992 election, an even more famous singer said she would move to England if George Bush was reelected president.

But our best-known national pessimist is Stanford biologist Paul Ehrlich. In 1970, he predicted that four billion people worldwide, including 65 million Americans, would die of hunger during the 1980s. An equally depressing 1972 Club of Rome report, titled "The Limits to Growth," blithely asserted that the world would begin to run out of critical raw materials in the 1980s. This in turn fired up Ehrlich again, who subsequently made a $1,000 bet with another scientist that market prices for five strategic minerals (copper, chrome, nickel, tin, and tungsten) would skyrocket between 1980 and 1990. Despite having to pay up when the prices of all five commodities went down instead of up, Ehrlich still refused to admit he was wrong about the imminent end of the world.

In my view, there is no reason for such pessimism, especially since all the evidence suggests that conditions are getting better almost anyplace you look. Although the world's population has doubled over the last fifty years, food production has tripled. The average life expectancy has increased by seventeen years over the last four decades. Infant mortality has been cut in half.[1]

When adjusted for inflation, a gallon of regular gasoline costs less than it did forty years ago. Air pollution is decreasing; smog levels even in Los Angeles have declined 50 percent in the last ten years. Rivers and lakes are cleaner. Salmon have returned in record numbers to our western streams. The tropical rain forest may be disappearing in Brazil, but in the United States the number of acres of forest land increases every year.

1. Ronald Bailey, "Seven Doomsday Myths about the Environment," *The Futurist*, January/February 1995, page 14.

Our future has never looked better. A few generations ago, by the time a person was sixty-five, his influence was on the wane. Travel was difficult. There was no such thing as mass communications. Today, people like Milton Friedman, the famous economist, pop up everywhere. His influence is undiminished. Technology, communications, and the ease of modern transit allow people like Friedman, who was born in 1912, to have more impact than ever before. Ideas are what matter. That's what makes the world move, not the ability to cut down trees faster with a handsaw.

Machines are the concrete manifestation of ideas, and ideas have impact. There is no reason to think we won't get better over time. Change is always a threat to some people. But over the long haul it becomes a positive thing. Sure, there will always be Unabombers and Wobblies. There are always people uncomfortable with new ways of thinking and doing.

Actually, the world has changed less in recent times than it did in our grandparent's generation. Think about the kind of technology people had in 1896: the telegraph, the steamboat, the railroad, and the knitting machine; that's about it. Then, over the next one hundred years the world industrialized. To people alive in the early part of this century, these changes came as marvelous, wondrous things—electric lights, automobiles, airplanes, and the surprising news that man really *could* fly.

Societies tend to alternate between periods of invention/ breakthrough and implementation/engineering. Today, we are in an engineering and implementation phase, in which we will see the use of technology that is here already. We aren't going to invent the transistor again. We aren't going to invent the jet airplane again. Whether a jet airplane goes 500 or 1700 mph isn't really the question. This phase should last ten years, during which time I think video telephone will play a part. Then another ten years will come after that, followed by another phase of breakthroughs. One hundred years from now, we very well might have instantaneous travel by molecular transmission through wires and fiber optics. "Beam me up, Scotty" may become a reality. Who knows?

We are going to see a lot of things that don't seem possible today, such as the integration of biology and electronics; people are already talking about biological computers. The two may be the same anyway—maybe our brains are just a bunch of electronic connections. In the meantime, we may destroy or discard industries built in the last one hundred years. We might not need automobiles anymore. We might not have an aircraft industry a century from now—why bother with physical transportation if we can just beam ourselves to, say, Kansas City?

One thing is certain: there won't be any lack of ideas. That is always what has been important—not muscles, not force, but brains and brainpower. That's the real human spirit.

The Dow Jones Industrial Average recently celebrated its one hundredth anniversary. There's only one company that was part of the Dow when it started and is still part of the Dow today: General Electric. Is GE the same company today it was a hundred years ago? Not on your life. The original GE was Thomas Edison's personal enterprise. It's a totally different world today.

Sure, when you look around you see things that look like crises in the short run. But these are transitory problems, and problems get solved—sometimes in surprising ways, by people or groups you'd never have expected to come forward with the answer.

For instance, look at how people are worrying about computer confidentiality. Who is going to keep the government from censoring, controlling, and regulating the Internet? I think the saviors are going to be the U.C. Berkeley nerds. The computer scientists understand the dangers of excess government, because they know that if the government ever cracks down they will be the ones the government will come after first. Most Berkeley grads tend to be on the political left, but when it comes to government intrusion, right or left has nothing to do with it—we're talking about individual freedom. They are going to be perceived as the real libertarians, the real freedom fighters. These people are a threat to big institutions because they are small. They are a threat to bureaucracy and administrations of any kind because they believe in freedom.

The world is changing. It's becoming hostile to big institutions and solicitous of individual freedom. That's what makes me optimistic. Sure, there will be bumps in the road, and it will never be a straight line. Are we going to have more wars? I don't know.

Countries that we currently see as our economic foes, such as Germany and Japan, may disappear into history. I don't mean to pick on them particularly—a lot of Europe has the same problem. They're run by people who think old.

There's a difference between being old and thinking old. Thinking old is the kind of thinking that is still predisposed to big, centralized governments. Germany has opted for a welfare-state socialism where nobody works and everybody gets paid anyway. In Japan, big corporations and big government are becoming interchangeable. That's not a role model for us and that's not a role model for the rest of the world. Japan has existed as a democracy for only fifty years. It's not clear whether Japan will become more like the United States or if it will go into its own shell.

Could Japan be a leader in information and new technologies? Sure. You don't need a resource-rich economy to provide information, services, and an interchange of ideas.

Will Japan do that? Maybe, but it is not inevitable. We'll have to wait and see.

China could be a major beneficiary of the next round of implementation. In fact, in some ways it could even jump ahead of the industrialized world. With cellular telephones and satellites, it is a lot cheaper for China—even though it might look expensive to us—to connect far-flung outposts.

Russia will have to decide whether it is going to be part of Asia or part of Europe; whatever it decides will cause it to break up even more. The railroad used to tie Russia together, but the railroad is old technology. The new technology basically says that the part of Russia that was China one hundred years ago will go back to being China; the remainder of Russia will remain European.

The United Kingdom has an opportunity to sit in the middle of these changes and play Who Do You Trust? The pound is still a very important currency to people in Arabia, Africa, and much of Britain's old empire. The UK can play the same role in Europe that the United States plays throughout Latin America, Canada, and Mexico.

Change is hard, but human beings can adapt to change. We have an instinct for freedom. Stifling political institutions have to be inflicted on us; they are not natural. My optimism really comes from the ability of the marketplace to overcome almost any adverse bureaucratic political control. Human beings are buoyant by nature. We pop to the surface; we rise. We keep coming up, and it takes constant pressure to keep us submerged. The intellectual elites can enforce repressive policies on the economy and on the citizens in this country, but they can't do it forever.

Again, time horizons matter. Is ten years really a long time or not? The Chinese know they have been around 8,000 years, and odds are they will be around another 8,000. What is ten or twenty years to them? This attitude might be of some use, but I'm not sure it helps them as much as thinking of themselves as young and vibrant. The U.S. has only been here 200 years. The State of California has been around for only 130 years. Until 1912, Arizona was a U.S. Territory, a fact that became an issue in Barry Goldwater's 1964 presidential campaign, when some people claimed that Goldwater hadn't been born in the United States and thus had no right to run for president.

How will the U.S. stay young? Will we acquire Canada and Mexico? Possibly. However, progress is not just a matter of age. It's a function of brainpower.

The mapping of the human genetic code is going to be completed far faster than anyone originally believed. Bright high school kids are today doing science projects that five to ten years ago people thought couldn't be done without spending billions of dollars and taking thirty years. Now we can hook up a powerful but cheap desktop PC and run it twenty-four hours a day. We've got the confluence of computing power and thought process. We've got machines that can do DNA sequencing around the clock; we don't need 10,000 lab coats working side by side. This kind of stuff is going on around the world.

If molecular transmission happens fifty or one hundred years from now, it will happen because someone who isn't even born yet will have dreamed up how to do it. Even that person won't be the one who makes it a practical reality. Change has to be accepted by middle-aged or older people, or it doesn't happen. The automobile did not just gain popularity among eighteen-year-old kids, but among people who could afford them and who understood the impact—middle-aged or older people. I'm not arguing that older people invent things. Most of the time we don't. But, by God, we are the implementers. We are the users. We know how to do things.

Some of my optimism comes from the fact that I am just naturally optimistic—it may be just as much a character trait as anything else. Even allowing for that, I don't think most people are optimistic enough about what can be done in the future. And I think they are too optimistic with today's values of financial markets. I see myself someplace in the middle—deliberately cautious about the markets, wildly optimistic about America and our future.

Glossary

Not everyone would agree on some of these definitions, but they describe how I use these terms in this book. Perhaps you ought to consider this section "Spare's Glossary" instead.

401k plan: A retirement plan offered by employers and funded through pre-tax payroll deductions; jointly financed by employee and company contributions.

annual dividend yield: Annualized dollar dividend divided by stock price.

annuity: An arrangement with an insurance company in which the individual gives a fixed sum of money and the company guarantees to pay the individual so much per month or per year, for a stated number of years or the rest of the individual's life.

appreciation: A rise in value or price over time.

asset: Anything owned that has exchange value; personal or business resources, as notes receivable, cash, inventory, equipment, and real estate.

asset allocation: The process of diversifying a portfolio by allocating portions to different asset types, such as stocks, bonds, real estate, and cash.

bear market: One in which the market is down approximately two-thirds of the time and up the rest; the opposite of a bull market.

beneficiary: The person named to receive the income or inheritance (cash, property, stock) from a will, trust, or insurance policy.

bonds: Interest-bearing certificates issued by businesses or the government, promising to pay the holder a specified sum on a specified (maturity) date.

bull market: One in which the market is up approximately two-thirds of the time and down the rest; the opposite of a bear market.

business cycle: Regular alterations of periods of prosperity and periods of depression.

cash: Ready money, including money on deposit.

certificate of deposit (CD):   A short-term debt security issued by a bank or savings and loan association usually with a maturity date and penalties for early withdrawal.

certified financial planner: A financial advisor with letters after his or her name.

cheap-stock investing: Value investing; buying stock when it is cheap (undervalued) and selling when it is expensive (overvalued).

cheap stocks: Value stocks; stocks thought to be in such serious trouble that investors abandon them, driving prices below what they're really worth.

compounding: A process in which interest is paid on the original investment plus accrued interest.

cyclical: Stocks whose revenues and earnings move up and down with the economy or occur in cycles, which occasionally causes them to be reclassified as growth or value stocks.

depreciation: A decrease in value over time.

discount: The difference between the cost of a treasury bill and its face value.

diversification: The distribution of investments among different types of securities to reduce risk.

dividend: A portion of profit per share paid to shareholders as decided by a company's board of directors.

dollar cost averaging: A method of stock buying in which the investor spends a given amount of money every month, regardless of the price.

Dow Jones Industrial Average (DJIA), or the Dow: Famous index of overall stock market performance; uses a group comprising thirty American multinational conglomerates and companies such as General Electric, Disney, Exxon, and Sears.

earnings: Profits.

equities: Shares of stock. Investments that convey ownership and allow the benefits of asset appreciation, not just interest or dividends.

fair value (fully valued):   A stock that's between cheap and
   expensive.

Federal Reserve System (the Fed):   Department of the
   government that runs the United States central bank,
   regulates credit, oversees the money supply, and
   sometimes sets interest rates for federal government
   securities.

government securities (treasury securities):   Treasury bills
   (T-bills), notes, and bonds.

growth stocks: Stocks with potentially above-average
   earnings growth rates.

income beneficiary: Person named to receive the income
   from the principal of a trust.

index mutual fund: Mutual fund whose performance
   parallels the market's performance.

inflation: An increase in consumer prices accompanied by a
   decrease in the purchasing power of money.

investment: Anything in which money may be invested for
   the purpose of obtaining income or profit.

investment advisor: A professional portfolio advisor.

IRA: Government sanctioned tax-deferred Individual
   Retirement Account, which allows a citizen to deduct
   $2,000 from earnings and invest it for retirement.

liabilities: Financial obligations; debts.

liquidity: The ease with which an investment can be
   converted into cash.

market capitalization: A company's total outstanding
   shares multiplied by its price per share.

market-capitalization-to-revenue: Market capitalization divided by revenues; a measure of a stock's cheapness.

maturity date: The date on which the full value (face value) of a security, such as a bond, must be repaid to the owner.

momentum investors: People who buy certain hot stocks, thereby driving up the price.

money market fund: A mutual fund that invests in short-term financial instruments, as treasury bills, commercial paper, and corporate securities.

municipal bonds: Securities issued by state and local governments and agencies, usually tax-deferred.

mutual fund: An account that uses funds obtained from shareholders to invest in stocks, bonds, and money-market instruments.

overvalued: Stocks that cost more than they're really worth.

portfolio: The sum of a single person or entity's investments.

portfolio management: Analysis of how best to position, diversify, or allocate an individual's investments.

price-to-earnings ratio (PE): The price of a stock divided by its earnings per share; a popular but generally inaccurate guide of value for investors.

principal: The main body of an investment or estate, as distinguished from income.

relative dividend yield (RDY): The dividend yield of a given stock compared to the yield of the market; a measure of a stock's cheapness (value).

remainder interests: The secondary beneficiaries of a trust, usually children or grandchildren; beneficiaries of a trust's principal when the income beneficiary dies.

revenues: The return from a property or investment; income; also a company's total sales, a more dependable measure of value than earnings (profits).

risk/reward ratio: Comparing the amount of risk taken in an investment to the reward gained.

securities: Documents or certificates indicating ownership of stocks or bonds.

Standard & Poor's Index of 500 (S&P 500):   An index of five hundred of the largest and most profitable companies in the United States.

stocks: Shares of a company.

total return: Total profit on an investment, plus appreciation and dividends.

treasury bills (T-bills):   Short-range government securities, usually maturing in ninety days to one year from date of issue.

treasury bonds: Long-range government securities, maturing in five to thirty years from date of issue.

treasury notes: Medium-range government securities, maturing in one to five years from issue.

treasury securities (treasuries):   Federal government bills, bonds, and notes.

undervalued: Stocks valued below their real worth.

value stocks: Cheap, or undervalued, stocks.

volatility: A measure of the likelihood that a stock or security may shift quickly and unpredictably in price; an investment's potential instability.

yield: Dividends divided by price.

Index